INSTITUTE OF INTERNATIONAL STUDIES
YALE UNIVERSITY

The *American People and Foreign Policy*

The Yale Institute of International Studies was organized in 1935 for the purpose of promoting research and training in the field of international relations. Although concerned with all aspects of international affairs, its studies have been primarily devoted to clarifying contemporary problems in the foreign policy of the United States. The members of the Institute work at all times in close association, but each member is free to formulate his research projects in his own way and each published study represents an individual analysis of a problem.

Publications of the Institute include: A. Whitney Griswold's "Far Eastern Policy of the United States," George T. Davis' "A Navy Second to None," Arnold Wolfers' "Britain and France between Two Wars," Nicholas John Spykman's "America's Strategy in World Politics" and "The Geography of the Peace," and Samuel Flagg Bemis' "The Latin-American Policy of the United States."

Other publications have been William T. R. Fox's "The Super-Powers," David Nelson Rowe's "China among the Powers," and Percy E. Corbett's "Britain: Partner for Peace." "The Absolute Weapon," written by members of the Institute and edited by Bernard Brodie, was a collaborative analysis of atomic power. The most recent volumes were William Reitzel's "The Mediterranean: Its Role in America's Foreign Policy," and Annette Baker Fox's "Freedom and Welfare in the Caribbean."

Frederick S. Dunn, Director

The American People
and Foreign Policy

Gabriel A. Almond

New York

HARCOURT, BRACE AND COMPANY

To Lisa and David Almond

"The joys of parents are secret . . ."

Contents

Acknowledgments

In his efforts to bring the resources of all the social science disciplines to bear on problems of American foreign policy and international relations, Frederick S. Dunn encouraged me to undertake the present study and spared nothing to facilitate its completion. At every point in the planning and preparation of this book I have had the advantage of wise counsel from William T. R. Fox. I am happy to acknowledge a long-standing intellectual debt to Harold Lasswell, who led the way among American political scientists in setting problems of political behavior in their socio-psychological context.

Others who read the manuscript in whole or in part and gave me the benefit of thoughtful criticisms are Percy Corbett, Jacob Viner, Bernard Brodie, Klaus Knorr, and Nathan Leites. Many errors and oversimplifications were removed through their friendly efforts. Those errors that remain are of my own making.

Violet Cook Lynch provided most generous and intelligent assistance in the research, preliminary drafting, and editing phases of the book. Mrs. Oliver Strunk of the Office of Public Opinion Research of Princeton University was very helpful in guiding us in the use of the Princeton collection of polling data. Anita Leonard Johnson gave the manuscript a final and sensitive editing, and Louise Brown Risk assisted in the proofreading. Veronica O'Neill, Barbara Mehl, and Mary Benedict shared the typing burden.

For permission to quote from works published by them I am indebted to E. P. Dutton and Company, Alfred A. Knopf, Inc., the Macmillan Company, The National Opinion Research Center, and The University of Chicago Press.

Bibliographical notes are to be found on pp. 245-258.

GABRIEL A. ALMOND

*The American People
and Foreign Policy*

I. World Leadership and Human Material

WITHIN a brief decade the American people have been torn from the privacy of civilian pursuits and thrust into a position of world leadership. A nation which by virtue of its geographic position and internal resources, its domestic institutions and traditions, had long rejected the strains of continuous participation in world affairs, has suddenly acquired a lonely and unwanted prominence. Like Atlas, it can find no shoulders to which to shift its burden. Moreover, it has come into its new status at a time when national security and foreign policy involve incalculable risks and costs. Reluctant to accept but unable to escape the responsibilities of world power, it is matched against an opponent which tends to subordinate all values to power, which accepts no limits to expansion, and no inhibitions as to method save expediency.

In our efforts to speculate intelligently about the outcome of this struggle it is difficult enough to calculate the objective factors such as economic and military power and potential. Even less susceptible to precise analysis is America's capacity for wise foreign policy decisions, its ability and readiness to use its resources in such a way as to maximize the national interest. Any comprehensive weighing of American prospects must place in the balance along with military and economic calculations an estimate of "psychological potential."

Ultimately, such an estimate involves an evaluation of

the entire field of policy in the United States since foreign and domestic policy are closely interdependent. Any action which affects American productivity and economic stability has foreign policy consequences as well as domestic. Similarly, the preservation of a relatively free economy and society in the United States is dependent on the politico-strategic situation in the world at large. Failure of American foreign policy in Western Europe, for example, cannot fail to result in greatly accelerated domestic mobilization measures and internal political controls.

An estimate of our capacity for intelligent foreign policy decisions also requires an understanding of the policy-making apparatus—popular attitudes toward politics which are conditioned by the "national character" and its regional and class variants, the system of indoctrination, education and information, the influential interest and pressure associations, the party system and the electoral process, and finally, the legislative and administrative establishments. In the American democracy control over policy is highly decentralized. But while power is widely distributed, a mass democracy obviously precludes the possibility of a direct and literal control of public policy by public opinion.

The treatment of problems of public opinion and foreign policy in the United States has been obscured and distorted by ethical bias and inhibition. All political systems have their myths, and democracies are not exceptions in this regard. The democratic myth is that the people are inherently wise and just, and that they are the real rulers of the republic. These propositions do have meaning; but if they become, as they do even among scholars, matters of faith, then scientific progress has been sacrificed in the interest of a morally satisfying demagogy.

A scientifically adequate approach to the problems of public opinion and public policy must begin with knowledge of psychic, social, and political structure and processes. This is the beginning of realism in the analysis of a democratic policy-making process. Opinions must be placed in their subjective matrices of values and basic attitudes if we are to gain an impression of their stability, ramifications, and possible future development. Opinions must be sociologically placed if we are to speculate intelligently about the potential political behavior of large social aggregations and their sub-groupings. Opinions and attitudes must be located in the political structure if there is to be any possibility at all of predicting policy developments from public opinion data. Finally, opinions have to be evaluated from the point of view of the objective problems to which they are a response.

If we examine any problem of public opinion and public policy with this type of structural analysis, the shortcomings of the democratic myth immediately become apparent. For example, can any people in the mass grasp with justice and wisdom the complex issues and strategies of foreign policy in the present era? Can any people in the mass and in the modern era make foreign policy in the specific sense of that term? The objectives which underlie such assumptions are inherently unrealizable, and by concentrating our attention on them we lose sight of the kind of popular control over public policy which is possible today.

There are inherent limitations in modern society on the capacity of the public to understand the issues and grasp the significance of the most important problems of public policy. This is particularly the case with foreign policy where the issues are especially complex and remote. The function of the public in a democratic policy-making process is to set certain policy criteria in the form of widely held values and expectations. It evaluates the results of policies from the point of view of their conformity to these basic values and expectations. The policies themselves, however, are the products of leadership groups ("elites") who carry on the specific work of policy formulation and policy advocacy. The public share in policy decisions may be compared, with important qualifications, to a market. It buys or refuses to buy the "policy products" offered by competing elites. However, the policy market is not as simple as an economic market. There is, unfortunately, no simple policy currency in which the costs of alternative policies can be computed. The policy products cannot be felt, tasted, or weighed. They are predictions of consequences of action, hardly a tangible product with regard to which consumer preferences can easily be registered.

In view of these considerations many of the moralistic exhortations to the public to inform itself and to play an active role in policy-making, particularly in foreign policy, have the virtues and failings of evangelism. This approach spreads the apocalyptic vision of a public, resolute and courageous, intelligent and informed, doing battle with vested interests, minority groups, or the power-hungry bureaucracy. But the resolution collapses with the next edition of the morning paper when the fall of another French government dramatizes the incapacity of the average man to understand the details of the distant world which shapes and conditions his fate. Such an approach as this fails to give due weight to the complicated structure of the policy-making process in a mass democracy, and attempts to impose a type of burden on the layman which he in most cases and in good sense rejects.

Public education ought never to attempt to make experts and specialists of laymen. Not expertness but improved understanding is the target which the public should be urged to set for itself, if progress is to be made in dispelling the fog of apathy and ignorance which facilitates the misrepresentation of the national interest. But such a program would have to start with more modest expectations and a more rigorous conception of social and political structure. It would recognize the awful proportions of a task which attempts to modify basic cultural, and perhaps human, predispositions and frailties. It would also have to place great emphasis on the training of specialized personnel, as well as on mass enlightenment.

Thus more advantage may be gained by the training of a few specialists in foreign affairs to serve on the staffs of the great interest associations such as the Chamber of Commerce or the American Federation of Labor, than by a half dozen short-lived experiments in community participation in world affairs. A well-trained specialist, able to devote full time to his particular field of policy interest, is in a position to inform and moderate the views of the leadership of his interest group, undertake the training and education of local officials, and institute informational programs under relatively favorable conditions.

Far greater returns may be expected from efforts to broaden the curricula of teachers colleges, theological seminaries, and schools of journalism to include sober studies of international economics and politics than from the more spectacular efforts of the "forums of the air." The problem is to introduce information and critical intelligence into the stream of communication at key points in the political process and in channels which conform to the "social terrain," [1] at points where trust and intimacy open the minds of men to new thoughts and recognitions.

The layman inevitably turns to his leaders for guidance on public questions. He can draw sound inferences and arrive at sober conclusions if he can trust his specialists to formulate the issues and alternatives in such a manner that a reasoned choice becomes possible. This is the task and the responsibility of the opinion and policy elites in a mass democracy. The layman ordinarily cannot formulate alternatives so that he can see how and in what way his interests are engaged. If his feelings are manipulated or his interests misrepresented, if he is continually shocked and terrorized, a sense of distrust of the entire policy-making apparatus develops. In some measure the problem of public apathy and ignorance might be solved if the political, bureaucratic, pressure group, and communications elites were governed by codes of conduct which minimized these elements of distortion and panic in the stream of communication. But to state this problem is not to suggest that deeply rooted cultural tendencies such as these can be remedied by short-run or spectacular measures. Given the bedlam which actually obtains, it is hardly an evasion of public duty if the ordinary human being shuts his ears and keeps a close hand on the wallet of his short-run interests.

From this viewpoint no sudden cultural maturation is to be anticipated in the United States which will be proportionate to the gravity and power of its newly acquired international status. The objective challenge of American primacy in world affairs will have to be met by present-day Americans with existing institutions and culturally imposed qualities of character.

This study is a structural analysis of American attitudes toward foreign policy. It does not merely describe the fluctuations of opinion but in addition seeks to relate them to the context of basic American attitudes, locates them in the social and political structure, and evaluates them in the light of the foreign policy environment of our time.

To this end the first step in the analysis is to describe the environment in which Americans have to make their foreign policy decisions. What are the peculiar difficulties and problems of decision-making in the era of the cold war? In this context the significance of specific American attitudes and behavior tendencies becomes clear.

The second step in the investigation is to describe historic trends of culture and character in the United States. From such an analysis of basic value patterns it will be possible to speculate about responses to present or possible future shifts in Soviet tactics, or to possible changes in the domestic American or world political situation. In the absence of tested hypotheses about the "American character" we have had to rely on the intuitions and impressionistic observations of historians, writers, and anthropologists.

The third task of the book is to describe shifts and fluctuations in mass moods and attitudes since the end of World War II and their distribution within the social structure. This section of the study is based on the enormous collection of foreign policy opinion material produced by commercial and academic public opinion research in the last few years. In the eager clamor of the 1948 post-election criticism of public opinion research, a simple fact has been overlooked. Despite its limitations and shortcomings, it still constitutes the most valid quantitative evidence available on mass attitudes and opinions. Its findings are used to answer such obvious questions as: What is the actual state of American opinion on the issues of foreign policy, and how has this changed since the end of World War II? The findings are also related to the earlier analysis of the foreign policy consequences of basic American attitudes and values. Do they tend to confirm or refute the more impressionistic analysis of American values and behavior? Do they support earlier predictive propositions about American vulnerabilities? Finally, these materials are used to differentiate the American audience into social sub-audiences characterized by special susceptibilities to the appeals of the various foreign policy elites.

The final task of the book is to describe the foreign policy elites—both structurally and ideologically. The plan is to proceed from the most general to the most specific, from the inarticulate cultural premises to articulate foreign policies at the elite level. We will then have before us as a basis for disciplined speculation about the American psychological potential: (1) propositions about basic American values and attitudes as they condition foreign policy moods among the masses and articulate foreign policy proposals among the elites; (2) propositions about mass moods on questions pertaining to foreign affairs, their fluctuations through time, and their distribution through "social space"; (3) propositions about the structure and the ideological characteristics of the American foreign policy elites and their articulate foreign policy proposals; and (4) propositions about the interdependence of these three levels of foreign policy opinion.

Such an analysis will make possible a number of observations as to the structure, composition, and planes of cleavage of American opinion in foreign policy matters, and as to possible future responses of American opinion to changes in the conditions of world politics. It will also be possible to suggest criteria of effectiveness which may be of value to those responsible for the formulation and execution of public information programs in the foreign policy field.

II. The Psychological Impact of the Cold War

DURING the nineteenth and early twentieth centuries a balance of power system protected the United States from the ugly facts of world politics. The prevailing moods toward foreign affairs tended in the direction of indifference, passive observation as of a game, occasional indulgence of idealistic or interest-oriented interventionism. Foreign affairs was not a discipline, not a regular part of the focus of attention. While in objective terms this world had certainly ceased to exist by the time of the first world war, a people whose primary genius lay in the elaboration of private values and material welfare persisted in its world of make believe until the bombs fell.

The world we entered after the recent war finds the United States more fully involved in decisions affecting international politics than any other country save Soviet Russia. Furthermore, it is an era overcast with risks and threats on a scale qualitatively different from anything which has gone before. What are the motives and impulses which drive us in the direction of involvement in world politics, and what are the aspects of the foreign policy environment which repel us, foster escapism, create inhibition, or seduce us into withdrawal?

Like the economists we may approach this question of involvement or withdrawal in terms of incentives and disincentives. We are involved in world politics because our basic aims and values are under attack by an expanding Soviet Union, and because we are the only power capable of resisting this expansion. The basic value orientation which we hope to foster by this involvement is an open system in which freedom, mass welfare, and peace can coexist. None of these values are absolute. Freedom may be limited in the interest of welfare, and welfare may be restricted for the sake of freedom. Peace may be subordinated to freedom and welfare, and immediate peace may be subordinated to ultimate peace. It is the preservation and expansion of this open, internally conflicting system of means and ends which is now under general threat on the part of a universalist, dogmatic-absolutist, monolithic Soviet Union. The desire somehow to deal with this threat at minimum risk and cost to our own value system constitutes the positive incentive for contemporary American involvement in world politics. Views of what comprises the positive American stake vary from class to class and group to group. But for the great bulk of the population some combination or interpretation of these values is what is fundamentally involved.

The foreign policies based on unambiguous efforts to foster the American and Western value system in the face of Soviet attacks may be characterized as rational interventionism. Here is a real threat to crucial values and interests, and here is an adequate policy to deal with this threat. But it would be a gross error to treat American interventionism as unambiguously rational in this simple sense. Intermingling and conditioning this rational positive effort at value preservation are many emotional responses which can only be understood in terms of psychological mechanisms. Thus, simple retaliatory impulses to Soviet provocations undoubtedly enter into the "American attitude toward Russia" and introduce emotional overtones which affect accuracy of judgment and economy of policy. In addition to this simple type of emotionality in foreign policy, it is clear that the Soviet Union and Communism provide obvious targets for the projection and displacement of hostile feelings deriving from quite different sources. These negative incentives might be termed irrational interventionism. They constitute disproportionate or displaced emotional pressures which, so to speak, shake the lens of the policy camera, blur the image, and create errors of perspective.

Assuming that in the net the threat to American values is sufficient to produce a strong and stable involvement in world politics, nevertheless there are significant aspects of the foreign policy environment which frustrate and weaken this will to participate and play a role. We may refer to these as the disincentives, the aspects of world politics which repel involvement. There are at least five aspects of the contemporary world situation which tend to have this effect, which lame the will to responsibility. One of the most obvious of these is the element of risk.

Risk

Active participation in foreign affairs has always involved the assumption of risk of serious dimensions. In the absence of a legal international order the ultimate support of "vital" interests is the use of force. In at least two respects the risks of American foreign policy choices have been drastically increased since World War II. First, the United States is no longer shielded by a balance of power which previously made it unnecessary to make explicit advance commitments. She can no longer wait to discover where her vital interests lie until they have been brought home by vivid demonstrations, as in the cases of World War I and II. She has the foremost position in the non-Communist world, and her economic and military pre-eminence places upon her a continuing burden of initiative. She is therefore under pressure to make conscious and deliberate decisions involving the definition of vital interests and risk of war. In an earlier time a less prominent position in the balancing of power made it possible to indulge moods until events forced them to harden into more or less consistent and conscious policies. *It is now enormously more difficult to avoid the advance formulation of policies involving the deliberate assumption of the risk of war.*

Secondly, the development of military technology during and since World War II has transformed war from a limited to an unlimited risk. Because of the fact that there was a rough proportionality between the means of diplomacy and means of violence, the nineteenth century military theorist could state: "War is politics pursued by other means." Given the values of the time, it was possible to make a rational selection of war as an instrument of policy. Its costs were bearable, and even defeat did not necessarily mean catastrophe. It was possible to make rough estimates of the prospects of victory and defeat and to predict the shape and character of the postwar world in the event of the one or the other outcome. This is by no means to say that mistaken estimates were not made. The significant point was that the great powers could approach calculations such as these rationally, as limited risks involving expendable values.

The development of atomic weapons is the culminating phase in the historic process which has wiped out this rational proportionality between war and other instruments of national policy. The decision to risk modern war may have to be made, but hardly in a mood of relatively rational expectation and with that feeling of "expendability" which reflects a balancing of the risks and the costs of resort to force. Such a decision involves a voyage into the night, in which traditional and humane shores have been left behind. The great mass of Americans is fully involved in private pursuits and in the conditions of peace, prosperity, and freedom in which this value orientation thrives. They are unwilling to confront in rational terms a decision which might place this private and civilian value orientation in the balance in the interest of survival. Policy-making with regard to the use of atomic weapons calls for a degree of dispassionate rationality of which relatively few men are capable. It is hardly surprising, therefore, that the typical attitude in the United States, instead of sober calculation, ranges from ironic horror to simple evasion and escapism.

The nature of the risk of modern warfare, of course, varies with the distribution of atomic weapons. In the present phase of great American superiority in the possession of atomic weapons, the risk involved in their use is not one of American survival, but of the undesired and unanticipated consequences—physical, economic, political, moral—of an atomic war conducted by the United States. The indiscriminate destruction of civilian life occurring at the outset of a war (and not at the end after long provocation as in the case of Germany and Japan) would constitute a serious moral obstacle. While it is not out of the question that a threat of resort to atomic war might force the Russians to give way, we can hardly count on such a withdrawal. The decision to issue such a threat would have to be backed up by a readiness to act on the basis of its rejection. So great are the stakes of the Russians and the Communist parties that even in the event of American superiority they might very well conduct a resistance that would require continued and large-scale destruction. The United States justified the destructiveness of the American air forces in World War II by the cruelties of earlier German and Japanese air warfare. In the present case the United States would initiate this type of warfare and carry it on against an opponent who perhaps could not reply in kind. Furthermore, the outcome of American victory would not mean the achievement of security for the American way of life in any simple sense of that term. It might mean that the United States had become the dominant world power, responsible for maintaining order, remedying the destruction caused by its action, feeding and re-equipping a world more devastated than that which survived World War II. If there is a threat of undue military influence and the development of the "proconsul" spirit in American policy today, such a threat would be multiplied many times by the necessity of maintaining more and larger-scale occupations after any such a "victorious" war. The economic costs and consequences of such a victorious preventive war might far exceed the costs and consequences of World War II. Thus, even in the present period of American superiority in atomic weapons, a preventive war might create a serious threat to the essential American values of prosperity and material well-being, political freedom, and the security and privacy of a "civilian society."

If even under these one-sided conditions the risks of atomic warfare are out of proportion to American aims and aspirations, once atomic weapons in sufficient numbers become available to the other side and once they have developed carriers capable of reaching the United States, the risk of foreign policy decisions assumes unreal dimensions for most of us. While men may have to make such decisions, the enormous risks might seriously interfere with rational calculations of value gains and losses.

The inescapable assumption of overwhelming risk—physical, institutional, and moral—is perhaps the most important aspect of the foreign policy environment as it impinges upon the minds and emotions of the American people. While it can hardly be said that the average citizen formulates these difficulties in such terms as the above, some sense of the extraordinary dimensions of the problem has seeped through to the "man in the street" with consequences which we will have the occasion to discuss in the chapters which follow.

Tension and Threat

The peculiar characteristics of the Soviet and Communist elites constitute an aspect of the world environment which makes exacting demands upon American character and intelligence. For our purposes the analysis of three tendencies may be sufficient to suggest the scope of the problem.

First, the Communist movement is led by full-time professional revolutionaries who set as their goal the establishment of Communist dictatorships throughout the world. Every group of any significance in the United States feels itself to be threatened by this movement. To make an obvious point, this is not a historically familiar type of power politics intended to achieve limited national aims. The very social structure of the non-Communist world is threatened. The believing Christian, the trade unionist, the democratic Socialist, the liberal, the conservative—all save a small sector of the population—experience Russian and Communist pressure as a grave threat to fundamental values. This is what gives the problem of foreign policy its special poignancy. For, while the provocation to risk war is great, the destructiveness of modern warfare raises overwhelming problems as to its use.

Secondly, the Communist movement practices a "permanent activism." The tension and the threat characteristic of the struggle of the Communists to impose their domination on the world has become a permanent part of the political environment of the era. The Communist movement by virtue of its political organization and ideology is in a state of constant tension, dynamism and pressure. The strong drive to relax from tension in the "civilian," multi-value, non-Communist world facilitates the success of Communist tactics. The outside world is slow to react to pressure; it acquires a counter-momentum late. And the counter-momentum seems to be dependent on the continuance of obvious and dramatic Communist pressure. Thus a deliberate Communist tactical withdrawal might seriously weaken the will to take adequate security measures. The use of "tactical" and "strategic retreats" is, of course, an established Communist technique; but even if the Communists are forced to withdraw because of the strength of the opposition to them, their very act of withdrawal might produce a psychological demobilization. The recent history of efforts at Western European unification is a case in point. The first official overtures for political unification came immediately before the Communist seizure of power in Czechoslovakia. The Czech coup gave these overtures an urgency which resulted in a greater readiness to make commitments. But the enactment of the European Recovery Program and the defeat of the Communists in Italy in the spring of 1948 apparently weakened the motivation for political and economic integration. The Berlin crisis in the summer of 1948 again provided incentives for unification. This suggests the difficulty, although not the impossibility, for the non-Communist countries of taking and holding the political initiative. They appear to be dependent to a significant degree on provocation in order to take effective measures of defense.

A third aspect of the Communist movement is the complexity and versatility of its technique and political methods. Its fifth columns are far stronger and more skillful than anything the Nazis could put in the field. Especially in France and Italy, but in the United States and England as well, they have infiltrated the trade-union movement. In Western Europe and the United States the trade-union movement has large popular support. It is impossible to lessen its powers and influence without provoking serious internal crises. What this means in countries such as France and Italy is that the Communists through the trade-unions are in a position to sabotage internal programs of economic stabilization and to undermine and weaken the pro-Western foreign policies of these countries. The problem of ridding the trade-unions of Communist domination and manipulation is one of extraordinary delicacy and complexity. A direct attack on the trade-unions would confuse the moderate left and would perhaps drive some of its elements into the arms of the Communists. Should the United States foster such a policy in Western Europe it would provoke serious resistance not only in Western Europe but in the American trade-union movement as well.

Here again the threat and provocation is great, but counter-action is frustrated by Communist methods. The Communists quite skillfully combine their use of trade-unions for political purposes with the representation of popular working-class grievances.

Similarly, the complex problem of the Communist parties in Western countries requires subtlety in its solution. There is great reluctance for reasons both of morality and expediency to suppress these organizations. The moderate left, and liberal conservatives as well, find it difficult to reconcile liberal-democratic values with the suppression of political associations. Even those who are fully convinced of the "alien" and subversive character of the Communist parties are troubled by the precedent which their suppression would establish for more indiscriminate political suppression. And even those who find it possible to think these issues through and decide that suppression is legally and morally justifiable, still have to face the question of whether such action might not result in more harm than good. We know that if the Communist parties are suppressed, they are prepared to operate with some effectiveness underground. In order to destroy a resolute and effective underground it may be necessary to set up some of the apparatus of a police state.

The problem is further complicated by the fact that the threat of Communism in Western Europe has brought to the surface and strengthened authoritarian, nationalist and fascist groups. Between the Communists on the one hand and the potential fascists or extreme right on the other, the moderate democratic camp is hard pressed. Our programs of aid in Greece and Turkey have provoked serious conflicts of conscience in the Western democratic countries. Should these bipolar tendencies in Western European politics intensify, we may have to choose between tolerating the spread of Communism in the key areas of Western Europe and backing narrow right-wing or authoritarian regimes.

All of these problems involve judgments and decisions which deeply trouble and continually thwart the conscience and intelligence of devoted democrats and constitutionalists. While the impact is considerably less direct and frustrating on the general population, the debates over these issues cannot avoid the creation of feelings of moral and expediential risk and bewildering complexity.

Constant tension and anxiety, then, appear to be the lot of those who concern themselves with foreign policy questions in the era of Russian and Communist aggression. Economic measures and other means short of violence are of limited effectiveness in dealing with a force which has already won such solid positions and which has proved itself to be so resourceful and unprincipled an opponent. And yet, resort to violence, or even the threat of it, raises the gravest problems of judgment that men have ever been called on to face.

Cost and Sacrifice

In addition to grave risk and permanent tension American foreign policy means cost and sacrifices. These are normally bearable in the degree to which they are limited and likely to bear visible dividends. The costs of contemporary foreign policy, in contrast, are continually increasing. There is no end in prospect, and there is no full assurance that they will accomplish the ends for which they are intended.

The European Recovery Program was represented to the American public as an essential measure of economic and political stabilization which would render Western Europe more immune to Communist infiltration. It was represented as a means which would contribute to peace and as a step which might, in a period of a few years, make further American aid unnecessary. It is now evident that something less than optimum achievement under the Marshall Plan will be forthcoming and that demands on American financial resources will continue long after the end of the four-year period. Since the European Recovery Plan has been enacted the United States has had to assume the additional financial costs of efforts to attain some measure of military security in the Western European area. At the same time, the claims of the Far East and other areas are being pressed with increasing urgency.

The United States is faced with generally increasing demands from the outside for aid to prevent Communist penetration at the same time that remilitarization is taking on major proportions as a competitor for available resources. Remilitarization not only involves economic costs and sacrifices, but through selective service already casts the shadow of the threatened human costs of American foreign policy.

The multiplicity of claims on American resources confronts American opinion with the continual problem of intelligent allocation. Is a billion dollars of Marshall Plan aid as productive of American security as a billion dollars in aircraft development and manufacture? Are the claims of the Far East as urgent as those of Europe? In any situation in which abundant claims press on scarce resources, the tendency is to rule out what appear to be the riskier expenditures in favor of the "sure thing." How sure can anyone be that the investment in Western Europe will actually produce a stable economy and sufficient military strength to resist a quick Soviet and Communist conquest? What is the value of an American investment in an area which at the present time is incapable of defending itself from Russian aggression?

The allocation of American security resources in the era of cold war involves choices of the greatest difficulty and complexity. Thoughtful decisions may perhaps reduce the risks and economize the costs; but such decisions when represented honestly do not make what is ordinarily understood as good propaganda. If they are oversold they backfire in disappointment and disillusionment. If they are not oversold they are vulnerable to unprincipled attacks. The general effect is that the public not only is confronted by issues and decisions which are in their very nature grave, difficult, and complex, but that these issues more frequently than not reach the public in the form of distortions and caricatures.

Complexity and Difference

The problem of rational decision in foreign policy questions has already been described as extraordinarily intricate. But in addition to the complexity involved in attempting to minimize risk, to confront unremitting tension and threat, and to weigh alternative costs with prudence, complexity is of the very essence of the substantive issues of contemporary foreign policy and world politics. The conflict between East and West cannot be contained in particular geographic and cultural areas, nor can it be limited to particular means. The United States is involved in conflicts which are taking place in every significant culture area in the world; and each decision has to be considered in its political, economic, psychological, and military implications. While we attempt to familiarize and accustom ourselves to Western Europe, the Far Eastern crisis confronts us with a new and strange set of cultural conflicts and policy problems.

There is a strong temptation to reduce the variety of all of these cultures to the simplified terms of a Russian-Western conflict. But a genuine diplomatic virtuosity in the United States cannot develop without a thorough understanding of the uniqueness of cultures and nations and their component parts. Each nation and culture reacts according to its special history, social structure, and values.

The problem is not simply one of understanding and accepting cultural and political differences, but (1) of understanding and accepting so many of them in so short a period of time; and (2) avoiding an automatic preference for those traits which seem to be most closely related to our own values, or avoiding an automatic rejection of those which seem to be in conflict with them.

The most obvious illustrations of this type of problem are the socialist movements of Europe and the fascist and corrupt right-wing movements of Europe and the Middle and Far East. The majority of Americans are hardly well disposed toward socialist ideas and practices. And yet the socialist movements of Great Britain, France, Germany, the Low Countries, and Scandinavia are indispensable allies in the struggle to prevent Communist penetration of Western Europe. If we alienate them we weaken our cause and may have to seek out support in movements and groups which present far graver problems.

The conflict of values involved in our Spanish policy is another case in point. It is an obvious temptation to seek the strategic advantages and political security of the Iberian Peninsula regardless of the characteristics of the ruling forces in those countries. But if we offer the same hand to socialists and liberals that we offer to fascists, we are asking for, and will receive, a snub. The problem of difference and complexity in the foreign policy of a democratic capitalistic power in a world of ideological, political, and cultural heterogeneity may perhaps be stated in terms of three criteria. First, we must acquire a sufficient detachment from our own values to be able to tolerate different ones. Second, we must learn to accept and respect some traits and characteristics which we definitely dislike and reject. Third, we must learn to reject certain qualities which attract us by offering a confirmation of our own prejudices, or an apparent security and strength.

"Instinct" and affinity are dangerous guides to go by.

An undiscriminating ethics of the Sermon on the Mount in relation to our allies or potential allies is for saints and not for statesmen. To detachment we must add discrimination; we must accept the fact that the maximization of our security and the values with which it is related will require an unending series of rational calculations in which the influence of likes and dislikes has to be held to a minimum.

While it is relatively simple to grasp the principles involved, the complexity of the reality in which they have to be applied renders general guides to action untrustworthy. The United States, in order to preserve its own values and institutions, is engaged in the task of forming the most formidable coalition possible to resist Soviet penetration. In this task it must endeavor to hold together nations, political movements, and social and religious groupings of all kinds. There are risks in attempting to make the coalition too broad, and risks in forging it too narrow. There is danger in tying it too closely to the United States, and danger in too loose a tether. The risks and dangers can only be held to a minimum by the most reliable knowledge of the interior workings of cultures, nations, and ideological movements.

Here again, these are the special tasks of elites of one kind or another—the diplomatic service, journalists, publicists, and scholars. But the bewildering variety of peoples, cultures, issues, and movements cannot fail to have some impact on broader masses of the population. The basic danger is that, when confronted by this range of exasperating complexity and subtlety in the world of foreign affairs, the public might prefer the certainty of bias and prejudice to the possibilities and probabilities of rational calculation.

Rejection and Hostility

Finally, the environment of world politics is not un-equivocally indulgent toward the United States. The spectrum of emotional reaction toward America ranges from outright moral assassination by the Soviet and Communist elites to a general distrust and ambivalence which affects the attitudes of most of the peoples of the world toward America. The problem may be put in these terms: the United States not only assumes massive risks, lives in a state of constant tension and alarm, is confronted by mounting costs, and is bewildered by a babel of exotic politics and cultures, but has assumed all these burdens, so foreign to its character and experience, in a world which does not reward it with affection or respect.

The propaganda of the Soviet Union, the satellites, and the Communist parties elsewhere minimizes the American role in the recent war. American military action and lend-lease are given a minor place not only in the liberation of Europe, but in the Far East as well. It is alleged that we not only did not put much into the actual fighting, but that the fighting was for base purposes—the grabbing of markets and the spread of American domination. American postwar policy is described as a mere continuance of the same sordid plan.

Within the non-Communist left, distrust of American aims and intentions is deep-seated. Some of these elements, following the Marxist interpretation of fascism, either fear, or are convinced of, an alliance of American free-enterprise capitalism with right-wing and fascist movements in Europe. They tend to see the United States in two guises; first, as a tireless enemy of socialism, ready to ally itself with any conservative or authoritarian force, and second, as a ruthless hunter of markets. That such views exist quite outside the scope of the communist movements is borne out again and again in polls of opinion in the various European countries in which large groups see in the Marshall Plan an American effort to bolster its own economy by developing European markets. American expectations of gratitude for sacrifices (which in the minds of most Americans appear to be motivated at least in substantial part by humanitarian and selfless considerations) are likely to be frustrated as a consequence of these mutual misconceptions.

But the United States is disliked and distrusted not only by the extreme and moderate left. Each social group has some special aspect of America which it fears or finds distasteful. Traditional conservative elements are hostile to the materialistic and mechanistic emphasis in American culture. Nationalists are jealous of American power. Sober and experienced men of affairs are fearful of American political amateurism and impulsiveness. And underlying the attitudes of practically all elements is the simple and understandable protest over a fate which brought America high and Europe low, which decreed riches for the one and beggary for the other, without regard to just deserts and national virtue.

The general distrust and unfriendliness which characterizes much of that part of the world which is outside the Communist orbit has not as yet made much of an impact on general American opinion. But it may in the future produce reactions of some significance for American foreign policy. As a hint of what might happen, we have only to recall that the strength of anti-Russian feeling in the United States at the present time is in some measure fed by a bitterness over Russian and Communist ingratitude. Even American conservatives during the recent war had found friendly words for "Uncle Joe," gave active support to lend-lease, and were ready to make concessions to Russian demands for security in the postwar settlements. The unequivocal hostility of Communist policy in the last years has turned these friendly actions and feelings into gall, and has produced reactions which may impede a flexible American policy toward the Soviet Union.

In the same sense, the American fear of "being made a sucker" may be activated by the "ingratitude" of the non-Communist world. This would tend particularly to be the case if the notion should continue to prevail that American aid is motivated by humanitarian rather than security considerations. If the aim is understood to be American security, then friendliness and gratitude are welcome but not essential responses. But if the aim is viewed as humanitarian, and rejection and unfriendliness are forthcoming, then the existing minority opposition to the various economic aid programs may come to be supported by a general revulsion of feeling. This prospect is less likely under conditions of Soviet and Communist pressure, but a tactical Russian withdrawal might bring these reactions to the surface.

The simple truth of the matter is that never perhaps in history has a people risen to such power in so short a time, nor has a people been called upon to exercise power under such unfavorable circumstances. There are, as we have already seen, powerful incentives to face and resolve these difficulties. The strongest and most constructive is the positive desire to protect and enrich the fundamental values of freedom, welfare, and security at minimum risk and cost to ourselves and the rest of the world.

What can be said about the basic traits and attitudes of the people which has been called to this historic task?

III. American Character and Foreign Policy

ATTITUDES and opinions toward foreign policy questions are not only to be understood as responses to objective problems and situations, but as conditioned by culturally imposed qualities of character. These largely unconscious patterns of reaction and behavior strongly influence the perception, selection, and evaluation of political reality. At the level of mass opinion these "psycho-cultural" characteristics condition patterns of thought and mood on foreign policy problems. At the elite level they affect patterns of policy-making.

In order to speculate intelligently about the influence of these basic traits on foreign policy, it is first necessary to examine and analyze the most important interpretations of the "American character." Before specific judgment about the effect of these qualities on American foreign policy attitudes becomes possible, it is first necessary to discover what qualities Americans are alleged to have.

In the present state of knowledge all generalizations about "national character" are hypothetical in nature. All that we can say about the observations of historians, journalists, anthropologists, and philosophers who have contributed the bulk of these observations is that they are the reflections of more or less disciplined observers, possessing to a greater or lesser degree the kind of intuition and empathy so essential to this type of speculation. Perhaps a greater validity will attach to those judgments and observations which frequently recur in the literature. The main aim of this investigation is to isolate these persistent themes and set them up as hypotheses which may help us to speculate intelligently about American attitudes toward foreign policy.

Perhaps the most sensitive and accurate observer of American political behavior and institutions was the French aristocrat and historian Alexis de Tocqueville. He wrote of the America of the early 1830's but with a prophetic perception of potentialities which makes much of what he wrote still applicable today. To de Tocqueville, America was the great political experiment of his time, the experiment of political and social equalitarianism. He attributed the distinctively American behavior tendencies to social equality and the social mobility which resulted from it.

In the traditional regions of the Old World, de Tocqueville remarked, the people are ignorant, poor, and oppressed, ". . . yet their countenances are generally placid, and their spirits light. In America I saw the freest and most enlightened men, placed in the happiest circumstances which the world affords: it seemed to me as if a cloud habitually hangs upon their brows, and I thought them serious and almost sad even in their pleasures." [1]

De Tocqueville associated this restlessness and dissatisfaction with two patterns of behavior which he described as peculiar to democratic America. The first of these is an extraordinary emphasis on worldly and private values and gratifications at the expense of public and spiritual values. The second is an extraordinary competitiveness. Of the first tendency de Tocqueville remarks:

"In their intense and exclusive anxiety to make a fortune, they lose sight of the close connection which exists between the private fortune of each of them and the prosperity of all. . . . The discharge of political duties appears to them to be a troublesome impediment, which diverts them from their occupation and business. . . . These people think they are following the principle of self-interest, but the idea they entertain of that principle is a very crude one; and the better to look after what they call their business they neglect their chief business, which is to remain their own masters." [2]

With regard to American competitiveness de Tocqueville writes:

"It is strange to see with what feverish ardor the Americans pursue their own welfare, and to watch the vague dread that constantly torments them lest they should not have chosen the shortest path which may lead to it. . . . They have swept away the privileges of some of their fellow-creatures which stood in their way; but they have opened the door to universal competition; the barrier has changed its shape rather than its position. When men are nearly alike and all follow the same track, it is very difficult for any one individual to walk quickly and cleave a way through the dense throng that surrounds and presses on him. This constant strife between the inclination springing from the equality of conditions and the means it supplies to satisfy them, harasses and wearies the mind." [3]

At the same time he recognized a tendency toward periodic outbursts of evangelism, when the souls of the American people

". . . seem suddenly to burst the bonds of matter by which they are restrained, and to soar impetuously to Heaven. . . . If their social condition, their present circumstances, and their laws did not confine the minds of the Americans so closely to the pursuit of worldly welfare, it is probable that they would display more reserve and more experience whenever their attention is turned to things immaterial, and that they would check themselves without difficulty. But they feel imprisoned within bounds, which they will apparently never be allowed to pass. As soon as they have passed these bounds, their minds know not where to fix themselves and they often rush unrestrained beyond the range of common sense." [4]

De Tocqueville thus detects a moral dualism in American character. Coupled with the intense concern for private, material welfare is a propensity for periodic moral and religious enthusiasm. And further, de Tocqueville with shrewd psychological insight points out that the anxiety and the futility of unrestrained competitiveness creates just this susceptibility to bursts of unworldly evangelism and enthusiasm. He foresaw a threat to American democracy resulting from this alternation of moods of intense, private self-interest and passionate enthusiasm. While in domestic policy common sense and an intimate knowledge of the issues mitigated the influence of these tendencies, in foreign policy the remoteness and complexity of the issues created a special danger. Here the instability of moods, "the propensity that induces democracies to obey impulse rather than prudence, and to abandon a mature design for the gratification of a momentary passion" [5] could have a relatively freer sway. It was fortunate indeed for the interests of the United States, concluded de Tocqueville, that it did not need a foreign policy, that "it is called upon neither to repudiate nor to espouse them [passions of the Old World]; while the dissensions of the New World are still concealed within the bosom of the future." [6]

Other observers of the America of the pre-Civil War period confirm some of de Tocqueville's observations, although none presented so coherent and comprehensive a psychological characterization. Francis J. Grund, a German observer who lived in the United States in the early 1830's, commented on the great emphasis on material success in American culture and the discredit attaching to material failure and poverty.

> "A man, in America, is not despised for being poor in the outset—three-fourths of all that are rich have begun in the same way; but every year which passes, without adding to his prosperity, is a reproach to his understanding or industry; and if he should become old without having acquired some property, or showing reasons which prevented his success . . . then I am afraid he will be doubly punished—by his own helpless situation and the want of sympathy in others. . . . Happiness and prosperity are so *popular* in the United States, that no one dares to show himself an exception to the rule. . . ." [7]

Grund also comments on the exclusive addiction to "business" in the United States at the expense of leisure.

> "Active occupation is not only the principal source of their happiness and the foundation of their national greatness, but they are absolutely wretched without it, and instead of the *dolce far niente*, know but the horrors of idleness . . . the Americans pursue business with unabated vigor till the very hour of death . . . the term of *rentier* is entirely unknown." [8]

Charles Dickens, on the basis of his first tour of America, made a number of observations among which two are especially worthy of comment. First, he was strongly repelled by the "universal distrust" which he described as "a great blemish in the popular mind in America." According to Dickens, social relations in the United States were marred by excessive mutual hostility and lack of confidence. As an illustration of this tendency he pointed to the unwillingness of able men to engage in political careers because of fear of character assassination, a point later elaborated by James Bryce. Dickens made no effort to account for this hostility; but it would appear to be a trait closely associated with de Tocqueville's "universal competition." If each man is imperatively bent on his private success in competition with all his fellows, the stability and confidence of personal relations can hardly avoid impairment.

Dickens also remarked on the standard of secular morality in the United States and its divergence from the accepted norms of Christianity. What especially troubled him was the apparent public approval given to successful rogues. He cites an imaginary conversation to illustrate the point.

> "He [a scoundrel who had gotten rich by questionable means] is a public nuisance, is he not?"
> "Yes, sir."
> "A convicted liar?"
> "Yes, sir."
> "He has been kicked, cuffed, and caned?"
> "Yes, sir."
> "And he is utterly dishonourable, debased, and profligate?"
> "Yes, sir."
> "In the name of wonder, then, what is his merit?"
> "Well, sir, he is a smart man." [9]

Both Herbert Spencer and Matthew Arnold were among the host of English observers in the post-Civil War period who offered analyses of the American character and spirit. The main burden of Arnold's critique was the absence of esthetic and spiritual distinction or "elevation" in American culture. He also comments that American men and women were extremely nervous because of excessive worry and overwork. The pace of life was too active. There was too little provision for relaxation and creative leisure.[10]

Herbert Spencer's characterizations were remarkably out of character for the philosopher of "Social Darwinism." [11] The British sociologist complained in a public interview and lecture in the United States of the "aggressiveness" of American behavior and of the "disregard for the rights of others." American life was a high pressure life. "Exclusive devotion to work has the result that amusements cease to please; and when relaxation becomes imperative, life becomes dreary from lack of its sole interest—the interest in business . . . the satisfaction of getting on devours nearly all other satisfactions." [12]

A few decades later James Bryce remarked on similar trends in American opinion. With respect to the tension, competitiveness, and nervousness of American life and its consequences for the level of political thinking in America, he observed: "The sense that there is no time to spare haunts an American even when he might find the time, and would do best for himself by finding it." [13] In a remarkable chapter entitled "The Fatalism of the Multitude" Bryce to an extent anticipated a hypothesis later developed by Erich Fromm and elaborated by David Riesman.[14] He describes the United States as a country

". . . where complete political equality is strengthened and perfected by complete social equality, where the will of the majority is absolute, unquestioned, always invoked to decide every question, and where the numbers which decide are so vast that one comes to regard them as one regards the . . . forces of nature. . . . Out of the dogma that the views of the majority must prevail . . . grows up another which is less distinctly

admitted, and indeed held rather implicitly than consciously, that the majority is right. And out of both of
these there grows again the feeling, still less consciously
held, but not less truly operative, that it is vain to oppose or censure the majority. . . . Thus, out of the
mingled feelings that the multitude will prevail, and
that the multitude, because it will prevail, must be right,
there grows a self-distrust, a despondency, a disposi-
tion to fall into line, to acquiesce in the dominant opinion, to submit thought as well as action to the encom-
passing power of numbers." [15]

Bryce viewed this tendency toward "band wagon" psychology in democracies as a source of political instability and
irrationality. After an election in which his candidate has
suffered defeat "the average man will repeat his arguments with less faith, less zeal, more of a secret fear that
he may be wrong, than he did while the majority was still
doubtful; and after every reassertion by the majority of its
judgment, his knees grow feebler till at last they refuse to
carry him into the combat." [16] Stable attitudes and opinions
rest on inner conviction, habit, or tradition. Movements of
thought in older social structures are obstructed by the barriers of class and status, but when each man tends to adjust
his opinion to the majority decision, or to the pressure of
numbers around him, opinion tends to become volatile, subject to sudden changes in mood and shifts in focus of attention and interest.

". . . they have what chemists call low specific heat;
they grow warm suddenly and cool as suddenly; they
are liable to swift and vehement outbursts of feeling
which rush like wild fire across the country, gaining
glow like the wheel of a railway car, by the accelerated
motion. . . . They seem all to take flame at once, because what has told upon one, has told in the same way

upon all the rest, and the obstructing barriers which exist in Europe scarcely exist here. Nowhere is the saying so applicable that nothing succeeds like success." [17]

Basing his observations on a painstaking analysis of American political parties, M. Y. Ostrogorski developed a number of themes about the American character, some of them original, some of them confirming the views of de Tocqueville and Bryce. He placed special emphasis on materialism, practicality, optimism, the preference for improvisation, and the hunger for fellowship. "In that new world which was a mine of untold riches for whoever cared to work it," wrote the Russian political theorist, "material preoccupations have engrossed the American's whole being." [18] The function of the state came to be viewed as solely that of assisting in the production of wealth. The enormous productiveness of the land and the availability of natural resources have created a pattern of materialistic improvisation. "Of all races in an advanced stage of civilization, the American is the least accessible to long views. . . . Always and everywhere in a hurry to get rich, he does not give a thought to remote consequences; he sees only present advantages. He is preeminently the man of short views, views which are often 'big' in point of conception or of greed, but necessarily short." The riches of America coupled with equality of opportunity have produced a "boundless optimism." This faith in success, that "things will right themselves," "is not only a general tendency, but almost a national religion. Next to the 'unpractical man' there is no one held in such contempt as a 'pessimist.' " [19]

But the equality and mobility of American life produce a loneliness and individual isolation which is uniquely American. The citizen of the Old World, for all his disadvantages, is anchored in social space. He has "moral support," a sense of belonging. "The American lives morally in the vagueness of space; he is, as it were, suspended in the air; he has no fixed groove. The only traditional social groove which did exist, and which was supplied by the churches, has been almost worn down by the incessant action of material civilization and the advance of knowledge." To meet this need the American creates artificial associations— "all revealing the uneasiness of the American mind assailed by a sort of fear of solitude . . ." [20]

Among the more recent "intuitive" analysts of American character, the French conservative Lucien Romier comes closest to presenting a systematic interpretation comparable to those of de Tocqueville, Bryce, and Ostrogorski. Siegfried and Brogan suggest this approach but they have mainly been concerned with the description of institutions and the development of policies.[21] Romier, writing from the viewpoint of a conservative European, attracted by American enterprise and energy, and repelled by its mass culture and materialism, formulated his conclusion in terms of a struggle between the European and American spirit.[22]

Among the various qualities which he lists Romier gives greatest emphasis to the "pace" of American activity. The most distinctive quality of Americans in his judgment was their *élan*, youth, rapidity of movement. America is a youth or child-centered culture; old age and death are pressed into the background. ". . . the American is a man who 'works fast,' who seldom shows finesse and blunders rather often into scrapes, which he is at any rate able to get out of with some spirit and much good humor. His devouring ambition is to get to the end of an affair quickly, and to make a lasting or profound effect is a lesser consideration with him." [23] Romier attributes to Americans a preference for action rather than reflection, speed or practical efficiency rather than depth, constant and lightning-like changes rather than enduring qualities.

He refers to the obligation to work and make money as socially and economically inescapable. The American is caught up in a system of incessant competition with efficiency and success as ultimate values. He points out that this "cult of practical activity" and "obligation to make money" is a matter of moral salvation rather than a product of hedonistic values.

Romier also attacked the American "mass market" orientation. The lack of American esthetic and intellectual subtlety, the superficiality and instability of American political opinion, he attributes to the pressure of the mass market, which rewards the sensational and well-packaged production and is indifferent to the more complex and profound creative effort.

More recent commentators have done little more than repeat and elaborate on points that had already been made by previous observers. What is especially interesting in this series of characterizations is the surprising consistency and agreement between the early and the later observers, suggesting, perhaps, that these patterns of behavior had asserted themselves at least as early as the beginning of the nineteenth century and had remained relatively stable up to the present time. Thus, Mary Agnes Hamilton in 1932 remarks on the tension of American competition and its negative effects on intellectual and political life.[24] Laski, in the years after World War II, speaks of the stress in America on practicality and immediacy and the anti-theoretical orientation even among American intellectuals. He refers to the "universal passion for physical prosperity," the prevalence of the "idea of the dynamic career," and the "zeal for individual accumulation" which has become a "whole-time job."[25]

Henry Steele Commager, after a much more exhaustive survey of the literature than that contained here, also was impressed by the consensus among foreign observers—coming from different backgrounds and writing at different times—as to American characteristics. It is of interest that his selection of recurring themes should coincide so closely with those discussed in the foregoing material.[26]

Psycho-Cultural Hypotheses About American Character

What distinguishes these earlier observations concerning American character from the hypotheses discussed below is that they proceeded largely from insight and intuition rather than from an explicit general theory of human behavior. The propositions presented by the psychologists and anthropologists are similarly untested observations, but they have the advantage of being derived from a considerable body of evidence as to the interrelationships between culture and personality. Thus de Tocqueville observed the tension involved in the American striving for success and attributed it to the absence of class barriers and the general equality of conditions. Mead and Gorer follow the process through, hypothetically, from social structure, to childhood experiences, to adult behavior. What would appear to a nineteenth century historian as discrete behavior patterns are seen by the "psycho-cultural school" as interdependent aspects of cultural values and structure and personality tendencies. Consequently, their observations have greater direction. If they isolate a behavior tendency they know where to look for its genesis; and from one behavior tendency they can formulate hypotheses as to what other behavior tendencies might be found in association with it. In the present state of knowledge this has both advantageous and dangerous aspects. To an intellectual a theory is a species of property and, in common with other property-owners, he is often somewhat careless as to the means used to defend it. The Marxist historians illustrate this propensity to mold and select reality to support propositions which have ceased to be hypotheses and have become sacred dispensations. The same criticism can be leveled against the Freudian interpreters of culture who have displayed remarkable, if unfortunate, ingenuity in pressing reality into a neat and preconceived frame. Consequently, while the psycho-cultural approach holds out the hope of a science of human behavior, its present production has to be taken with a great deal of caution.

Three anthropologists have recently offered interpretations of the American character—Margaret Mead, Geoffrey Gorer, and Clyde Kluckhohn.[27] Margaret Mead comments at great length on the success ethic of American culture. She ascribes its origins to the family pattern in which affection is accorded to or withheld from the growing child in the degree to which it fulfills achievement norms. Affection is not accorded to the child in principle but in relation to performance. As a consequence the American places an extraordinary premium on achievement; he measures his worthiness or unworthiness first by parental responses, and later by community responses.

Two things might therefore be said about the American success imperative: (1) the emotional force of the propulsion toward success is strongly compulsive since the stake involved is the individual's fundamental sense of self-esteem and worthiness; (2) the criterion of achievement is not lo-

cated in the self but in the responses of others—parents and
the parent-surrogates of adult life. These hypotheses of
Margaret Mead are quite similar to Karen Horney's concepts of "compulsive competitiveness," and "the neurotic
need for affection." [28] Horney argues that the competitiveness of modern culture places the individual in a state of
hostile tension with his fellows which affects all personal
relationships, those between parents and children, between
parent and parent, between siblings, and between adults in
their business and social relationships. Self-esteem is dependent upon the evaluations of others according to a culturally defined success-failure scale. ". . . under the pressure of the ideology, even the most normal person is constrained to feel that he amounts to something when successful, and is worthless if he is defeated." The emotional isolation consequent upon this pervasive hostility "provokes
in the normal individual of our time an intensified need for
affection as a remedy." [29] This theme is also developed by
Erich Fromm in an historical and ideological context.[30]

A second point made in Mead's analysis is the peculiar
attitude toward authority which she attributes to the predominantly immigrant origins of the majority of Americans.
A large proportion of Americans, she argues, have in the
course of the past few generations gone through the experience of rejecting the cultural patterns of foreign parents.
This common experience has tended on the one hand to
undermine the strength of tradition and to weaken authority, and on the other to produce strong conformist tendencies. The particular processes which seem to be involved
here are the following: the American rejects and discredits
parental authority, and to some extent carries over this
attitude toward all institutional and personal authority.
Thus, in his competition with others for success and achieve-

ment he lacks stable traditional standards to which to conform. Similarly, his standards of achievement have no internal stability. He is dependent from childhood to adulthood
on external reassurance. The American consequently is in a
constant process of breaking with the past and conforming to
transitory norms, fashions, and fads. He is an anti-tradi-
tionalist and a conformist at the same time, illustrating a
type of ambivalence which possibly lies at the root of the
hectic restlessness which troubled European observers from
de Tocqueville to the writers of the present day. Mead
places the immigrant origins of most Americans at the center
of this iconoclastic-conformist dualism. De Tocqueville attributed it to competitiveness and the equality of conditions
of the American people. It is, of course, both factors taken
together. What Horney, Fromm and Mead have done is
to trace this and other tendencies from aspects of the culture, to patterns of child rearing in the family, to adult
behavior.

A third proposition of Mead's has to do with American
optimism. The American is ready to tackle any problem
with the expectation that he can bring it to a swift conclusion. In this, he places his trust in improvisation and tends to
reject complicated planning. He has extraordinary faith
in good will and effort in the solution of all kinds of problems—personal and political. Because of the simplicity of
his assumptions, and the lack of appreciation of the difficulties involved in many problems, this type of American improvisation is open to frequent disappointment and frustration. American action has tremendous *élan* which often
works wonders, but when it doesn't work and when secondary improvisations are similarly thwarted, the bubble of
optimism often collapses and gives way to moods of de-
featism and deflation. Americans tend to reject the kind of

sober reflection and calculation which might protect them from these shifts of moods.

A fourth point of Margaret Mead's has to do with the American attitude toward violence and aggression. Aggressiveness in general, she argues, is positively valued in American culture. Americans, from childhood on, tend to be encouraged to forward themselves and their interests without equivocation. But resort to force is ringed round by restraints. In the American family bullying behavior is inhibited by shame, and arbitrary resort to force is negatively evaluated. Force becomes morally usable in the event of attack. This does not imply an absence of combativeness. On the contrary the "chip on the shoulder" psychology which Mead emphasizes very often reflects an attitude of spoiling for a fight. But there would appear to be strong inhibitions against being the first to engage in a violent action.

Gorer's analysis of American character admittedly incorporates some of the main ideas of Margaret Mead. In certain respects his analysis is extreme and distorted. Thus, he attributes a degree of anti-authoritarianism to Americans which does not seem to accord with reality. Americans certainly are distrustful of authority and are eager to limit it by checks and restrictions, but it can hardly be said that "Authority over people is looked on as a sin, and those who seek authority as sinners." [31] A case may be made out that arbitrary authority is viewed as evil, but it is difficult to believe that authority, in principle, has this connotation in America. At the same time Gorer has made some slight improvements on Mead's interpretation of the American pattern of authority. Mead lays extraordinary stress on the rejection of the immigrant father as a source of American anti-authoritarianism. Gorer probes more deeply into American political and social history and places the problem in the broader context of American political and social tradition.

Gorer stresses the moral dualism in American culture, the conflict between Christian ethical standards, and the ethics of the "market-place." In an ingenious and imaginative chapter entitled "Mother-land" he points out that American iconography includes two symbols—the shrewd, horse-trading Uncle Sam and the magnanimous Goddess of Liberty. "They represent in the shorthand of symbolism, a most important psychological truth. America in its benevolent, rich, idealistic aspects is envisaged (by Americans) as feminine; it is masculine only in its grasping and demanding aspects." [32] Like so many of his shrewd intuitions Gorer fails to carry his analysis through in a consistent and convincing fashion. He attributes the American tendency to cover all actions by some kind of moral rationalization to this maternally inculcated "idealism." But, if the American mother, as he alleges, is the dominant factor in the character development of children, and if the main burden of her influence lies in this idealistic, magnanimous direction, why, as he points out himself, should this idealistic factor in the "American conscience" affect behavior only superficially and mainly by requiring moral rationalizations for conduct that is based on quite different, and even contradictory, motives? Actually, the "American conscience" is a good deal more complicated than Gorer recognizes. While the American mother may typically be the most important child-rearing agent, it would seem to make more sense to view her as the bearer of both the "idealistic" and the "competitive" ethic.

In his treatment of the American emphasis on success Gorer points out that while money-making is the main criterion of achievement, there is little stress on accumulation for its own sake. "Americans will give their money with the greatest generosity, and not merely out of their superfluity: in many cases such gifts are made at the expense of considerable personal sacrifice." [33] At the same time this generosity is balanced by a "fear of being played for a sucker." Consequently, any action involving American generosity will be affected by this ambivalence. An underlying suspicion will require frequent reassurance that American gifts and contributions are not going "down the drain," or down a "rat hole," and that American good will is not being cynically exploited.

In briefer and more systematic form Clyde and Florence Kluckhohn summarize many of the propositions which have been discussed above. They also propose a number of original suggestions and elaborations. Thus they stress the American tendency to reduce problems to naively rational terms. The assumption tends to be made that any problem can be resolved by reasonable discussion and the "personal" or direct approach. Another element in this particular pattern is the belief in simple answers and the distrust and rejection of complex ones. The American tends to be anti-expert, anti-intellectual; there is faith in the simple rationalism of the "Average Man." [34]

This anti-intellectualism, according to Kluckhohn is mainly limited to ideas and problems pertaining to personal and group relations. There is no such inhibition to sustained thought and complicated reasoning in matters pertaining to material culture. Thus the enormous development of American technology, and the great stress on labor-saving gadgets. Indeed there appears to be a strong tendency to reduce more complex social and political problems to the simple dimensions of technical gadgetry. Americans often act as though political and cultural problems are capable of being mastered by ingenious schemes.[35]

A number of general points may be made with regard to the propositions which have so far been advanced as to characteristic patterns of behavior among Americans. First, it is essential to stress again and again that the material is highly speculative. Research is only in its beginning phases, and there is evidence to suggest that many of the writers in this field have jumped to interpretation without giving any evidence of having seriously confronted the extraordinarily difficult methodological problems involved.[36] A certain atmosphere of euphoric amateurism, which perhaps marks the earlier stages of all new scientific ventures, still beclouds the psycho-cultural approach. It will be dispelled only by thoughtful self-criticism which results from careful empirical research, cautious interpretation of findings, and the development of theoretical sophistication.

It does not follow, however, that we must suspend use of materials of this kind until genuinely valid observations are available. To the extent that they can be made relevant to problems of public policy, they are a good deal better than "hunch" or "rule of thumb" propositions about possible reactions of Americans to policy problems of one kind or another. Then again, it is possible to distinguish those "traits" which are referred to frequently in the literature over a period of many decades. The fact that successive generations of observers tend to reach similar conclusions suggests a greater credibility. In addition, some propositions seem to have an inherent plausibility, as tending to agree with informal observation, while others convey the impression of gifted, if untrustworthy, fantasy or theoretical presuppositions which have focused attention on particular phenomena regardless of their connection or representativeness.

In the systematic inventory which follows we have made an effort to include only those observations which have continually recurred and those which seem to have an inherent plausibility, recognizing that the criterion of "plausibility" is a purely subjective one.

1. General Value Orientation

The characteristic American value orientation would appear to consist of the following interrelated traits.

a. The degree of atomization in the United States is perhaps greater than in any other culture. The American is primarily concerned with "private" values, as distinguished from social-group, political, or religious-moral values. His concern with private, worldly success is his most absorbing aim. In this regard it may be suggested by way of hypothesis that in other cultures there is a greater stress on corporate loyalties and values and a greater personal involvement with political issues or with other-worldly religious values.

b. The "attachment" of the American to his private values is characterized by an extreme degree of competitiveness. He views himself and his family as in a state of competition with other individuals and families for success and achievement. American culture tends to be atomistic rather than corporate, and the pressure of movement "upward," toward achievement, is intense. Here again a hypothesis might be proposed that in other cultures individual competition for success tends to be more localized within specific classes or regions, tends to be subordinated to, or assimilated in, political competition, and tends to be muted by religious conceptions of life.

c. The American views himself and his family as in a state of competition with other individuals and families for values which are largely "material" in character. What he appears to want are the material evidences of success—money, position, and the consumer-goods of the moment. While the stress is toward money, or what money can buy, the important thing is not the money itself, but the sense of accomplishment or fulfillment which it gives. This sense of accomplishment rests on matching and exceeding the material standard of community and social class; it requires external approval and conformity. Because of the stress in the American value system on having what others want, and because of the great emphasis on the elaboration of material culture, the American tends to be caught up in an endless race for constantly changing goals—the "newest" in housing, the "latest" in locomotion, the most "fashionable" in dress and appearance. This love of innovation, improvement, and change tends to be confined to the material culture. Attitudes toward human and social relations tend to be more conservative. By way of hypothetical comparison it may be said that in other cultures the criteria of accomplishment are more stable. Religious salvation and political resentment provide greater consolation for the poor and the failures. The material culture tends to be hemmed in by tradition. The criteria of achievement have a more stable subjective basis in the sense of craftsmanship, esthetic and intellectual subtlety, and the fulfillment of social and religious routines.

d. There are certain derivative elements of this general value orientation which call for comment. First, intense individualistic competitiveness, in which the primary aim is to get more of what other people want, produces diffuse hostile tension and general apprehension and anxiety, which pervades every aspect of the culture including the competing unit itself, the family. The fear of failure and the apprehension over the hostility which is involved in one's relations with other persons produce on the one hand an extraordinary need for affection and reassurance, and on the other, an extraordinary tendency to resort to physiological and spiritual narcosis. In other words, as a consequence of being impelled by cultural pressure toward relationships in which one is aggressively pitted against others, the resulting unease and apprehension is characteristically mitigated by demands for external response, attention, and warmth, or by resort to escapism. Thus an excessive concern with sexuality, an excessive resort to alcohol, and, what is a uniquely American form of narcosis of the soul—the widespread addiction to highly stimulating mass entertainment, the radio, movies, comics, and the like—provide culturally legitimate modes of discharging hostility and allaying anxiety.

Thus, by way of summary, the value orientation of the American tends to be atomistic rather than corporate, worldly rather than unworldly, highly mobile rather than traditional, compulsive rather than relaxed, and externally directed rather than autonomous. Needless to say, these are presented as hypothetical tendencies, which are supported only by an inadequate and quite heterogeneous body of evidence.

2. *Value Expectations*

The American is an optimist as to ends and an improviser as to means. The riches of his heritage and the mobility of his social order have produced a generally euphoric tendency, that is, the expectation that one can by effort and good will achieve or approximate one's goals. This overt optimism is so compulsive an element in the American culture that factors which threaten it, such as failure, old age, and death, are pressed from the focus of attention and handled in perfunctory ways.[37] This belief that "things can be done" is coupled with a faith in common sense and "know-how" with regard to means. The American has a double approach to complex reasoning and theory. He has great respect for systematic thinking and planning in relation to technological and organizational problems. But even this type of intellectualism is brought down to earth by referring to it as "know-how." Know-how implies both the possession of formal technical knowledge and the capacity to improvise and overcome obstacles on the basis of a "feel" for the problem or the situation. In complicated questions of social and public policy there is a genuine distrust of complex and subtle reasoning and a preference for an earthy "common sense." Thus, in these important areas his compulsive optimism, his anti-intellectualism, and his simple rationalism leave the American vulnerable to deflation and pessimism when his expectations are thwarted and when threats and dangers are not effectively warded off by improvisations. This vulnerability is, to be sure, balanced by a certain flexibility and experimentalism, a willingness to try new approaches. If Americans typically avoid the rigidity of dogma in dealing with new problems, they also typically fail to reap the advantages of thoughtful policy-planning. What is involved here is not so much a net loss, but rather the failure to realize the net gain that would result from a greater intellectual discipline.

3. Attitudes Toward Authority and Morality

The American tends to "cut authority down to his own size." He has a respect for achievement and a toleration of order-enforcing agencies, but a distrust of arbitrary or traditional authority. This attitude toward authority also carries over into the field of tradition and custom. Certainly the urban American, and many of the rural ones as well, are not seriously limited by traditional methods of doing things. They are iconoclasts with respect to earlier aspects of culture, and conformists in relation to the most recent value changes. They reject what was done in the past, and they conform to the new things that are being done *now*. But again this iconoclasm is especially noticeable in the sphere of material culture. A greater conservatism obtains in relation to social and political matters. This social and political conservatism is not unique to Americans. What seems to be unique is this combination of mobility of material values and fundamentalism with regard to social and political values.

Similar trends are observable in American attitudes toward moral norms. The norms of Christianity still constitute an important theme in contemporary American culture. Since these moral standards are in obvious and continual rivalry with the competitive ethic, Americans tend to suffer from ambivalence and conflicts in determining what is "proper." Under normal circumstances this conflict does not appear to have a seriously laming effect. It tends to be disposed of by adding a moral coloration to actions which are really motivated by expediency, and an expediential coloration to actions which are motivated by moral and humanitarian values. These tendencies are related to a rather widespread naive belief in the compatibility of morality and expediency.[38] While this ambivalence is a factor which generally affects American behavior, there is also a characteristic pendulum movement between the two ethics. Thus, if generous actions, motivated by moral and humanitarian considerations, are accepted without gratitude, are misinterpreted, or are unrequited, a "cynical" rejection of humanitarianism may follow, resulting from the humiliation at having been "played for a sucker." To yield to humanitarian impulses in the "market place" or to moderate one's own demands in the light of "Christian" considerations, to give without the expectation of receiving, to suffer injury without retaliation—these are impulses which have a partial validity; but it is dangerous to give way to them since they dull the edge of competitiveness, confuse and retard the forward course of action.

Mood Versus Policy

Since Americans tend to exhaust their emotional and intellectual energies in private pursuits, the typical approach to problems of public policy is perfunctory. Where public policy impinges directly on their interest, as in questions of local improvements, taxation, or social security policy, they are more likely to develop views and opinions resting on some kind of intellectual structure. But on questions of a more remote nature, such as foreign policy, they tend to react in more undifferentiated ways, with formless and plastic moods which undergo frequent alteration in response to changes in events. The characteristic response to questions of foreign policy is one of indifference. A foreign policy crisis, short of the immediate threat of war, may transform indifference to vague apprehension, to fatalism, to anger; but the reaction is still a mood, a superficial and fluctuating response. To some extent American political apathy is a consequence of the compulsive absorption of energy in private competitiveness. To inform oneself on public issues, to form policies on the basis of careful thought-taking, is hardly a task that is beyond the intellectual competence of a large proportion of the population. The intellectual demands of business life are in some respects as complicated as those of foreign policy. But the American has a powerful cultural incentive to develop policies and strategies relating to his business and professional career, and little incentive, if any, to develop strategies for foreign policy.

The orientation of most Americans toward foreign policy is one of mood, and mood is essentially an unstable phenomenon. But this instability is not arbitrary and unpredictable. American moods are affected by two variables: (1) changes in the domestic and foreign political-economic situation involving the presence or absence of threat in varying degrees, (2) the characterological predispositions of the population. Our knowledge of American character tendencies, meager as it may be, makes it possible to suggest potential movements of opinion and mood which may have significant effects on foreign policy.

1. Withdrawal-Intervention

Given the intense involvement of most Americans with private interests and pursuits, the normal attitude toward a relatively stable world political situation is one of comparative indifference and withdrawal. This was the case throughout the greater part of the nineteenth century, in the period between World War I and II, and as we shall show in a later chapter, in the period immediately following World War II. The existence of this cyclical withdrawal-intervention problem suggests at least two serious dangers for foreign policy decision-making: (1) possible overreactions to threat; (2) possible overreactions to temporary equilibria in world politics. Under ordinary circumstances American emotion and action are directed with considerable pressure in the normal orbits of private competition. However, when threats from abroad become grave and immediate, Americans tend to break out of their private orbits, and tremendous energies become available for foreign policy.

Thus, we see the explosions of American energy in World Wars I and II when, after periods of indifference and withdrawal, exceptional feats of swift mobilization were achieved. There is some evidence to suggest that the Russian threat may, if carelessly handled, produce dangerous overreactions. Thus the press conference of Secretary of State Marshall in the spring of 1947, in which he urged the American people to "keep calm," produced what amounted to a war scare. The volatility and potential explosiveness of American opinion must be constantly kept in mind if panic reactions to threat are to be avoided.

The danger of overreaction to threat is only one aspect of this withdrawal-intervention tendency of American opinion. Equally serious is the prospect of overreaction to temporary stabilizations in the world crisis. Because of the superficial character of American attitudes toward world politics, American opinion tends to react to the external aspects of situations. A temporary Russian tactical withdrawal may produce strong tendencies toward demobilization and the reassertion of the primacy of private and domestic values. The pull of "privatism" in America creates a strong inclination to self-deception. And while this is less characteristic of the informed and policy-making levels, it undoubtedly plays an important role here as well. The great American demobilization of 1945, both in the military establishment and in the civilian bureaucracy, and the hasty dismantling of war agencies and controls reflected the overwhelming eagerness to withdraw to private values and normal conditions. This movement was not based on a sober evaluation of the foreign situation and what this might require in military and political terms, but was a response to the overwhelming urge to have done with alarms and external interruptions and get back to the essential and important values.

2. Mood-Simplification

Closely connected with the withdrawal-intervention pattern is a tendency which has to do with characteristic changes in the internal structure of American foreign policy moods. It has already been pointed out that under conditions of political equilibrium American attitudes toward world politics tend to be formless and lacking in intellectual structure. We define policy, as distinguished from mood, as consisting of a relatively stable intellectual structure including (1) explicit assumptions as to the values involved in domestic or international political conflict, (2) explicit evaluations of the relative costs and efficiency of alternative means of maximizing the value position of one's own country or political group. From the point of view of this criterion, American attitudes tend to range from unstructured moods in periods of equilibrium to simplification in periods of crisis. So long as there is no immediate, sharply defined threat, the attitude is vague and indefinite—e.g., apathetic, mildly apprehensive, euphoric, skeptical. When the crisis becomes sharpened American responses become more specific. Here American distrust of intellectualism and subtlety, the faith in "common sense," and the belief in simple answers lead to oversimplications of the threat and the methods of coping with it.

While these tendencies are more characteristic of the "uninformed" general run of the population, they affect policymakers as well. Thus during World War II, the Roosevelt shift from "Dr. New Deal" to "Dr. Win-the-War" reflected this need at the very highest level of policy-making to reduce the issues to simplified proportions. The "unconditional surrender" policy was a similarly oversimplified resolution of the moral and political problems of the war.[39] The journalists and writers who directed American propaganda efforts in World War II solved their complex policy problems by the slogan of "the strategy of truth," which left to the lower-level, competitive policy-making process practically all of the important decisions of propaganda policy during the war. The policy of "non-fraternization" with Germans which was imposed on the American army of occupation similarly was understandable as a gratification of a need for moral simplism, but it bore only a slight relation to the complex and uncomfortable realities on which it was imposed. The entire sequence of American policies toward Germany had this character of mixed moral-expediential improvisations. At first these improvisations were motivated primarily by anti-German reactions; more recently the tendency is toward more pro-German improvisations. At the present time this tendency to oversimplify seems to be taking the form of reducing all the problems of world politics to a simple "East-West" conflict. There is considerable pressure to take as an ally any country or movement which is anti-Communist and anti-Russian.

It would, of course, be an exaggeration to attribute the same degree of "simplism" to policy-makers as might be expected of the "man in the street." But there can be little doubt that the process of foreign policy making is strongly influenced by this common-sense, improvisation tendency. Faith in policy-planning (which means in simple terms, taking the "long view," acquiring sufficient reliable information on which sound policy can be based, weighing and balancing the potential value of military, political, diplomatic, and psychological means in relation to proposed courses of action) has hardly taken root in the American policy-making process.

3. Optimism-Pessimism

The problem of shifts in mood from euphoric to dysphoric expectations is clearly related to those aspects of American opinion already described. The involvement in private concerns, coupled with an optimistic faith in good will, common sense, and simple answers, renders the American public vulnerable to failure. This reaction tends to result from the frustration of successive improvisations, none of which have been adapted to the complex character of the problem. Under these circumstances there are two possible dangers: (1) withdrawal reactions; (2) hasty measures motivated by irritation and impatience. The development of American attitudes toward Russia since the end of the war is an excellent illustration of this problem. During the war and in the period immediately following its termination there was a widely shared belief among Americans and among American policy-makers that the Russian problem could be readily solved by good will and the "man-to-man" approach. The continued thwarting of American overtures and concessions to the Russians now seems to have produced an attitude of hopeless pessimism. Pessimism certainly seems to be justifiable on the basis of the facts, but the negativism which has resulted may possibly constitute a danger if negotiation and bargaining with the Russians in principle is interdicted. The objective problem would seem to be one of choosing the time, the occasion, and the conditions when negotiation might lead to advantage. There is a similar danger of excessive pessimism in relation to potential allies. Perhaps there is a tendency toward a premature "writing off" of peoples whose social and political structures are unstable, countries which don't react with "American speed" to American proposals or which are not ready to commit themselves to the American "side" in as whole-hearted a fashion as we might desire.

4. Tolerance-Intolerance

The point has already been made that the American attitude toward authority, toward moral and ideological norms, contains conflicting elements. On the one hand, the American is not hemmed in by the mores and morals of "the horse and buggy days," and at the same time he is a conformist, a value-imitator. He is ready to try new things and new methods, but not if they make him look "different" or "peculiar." The truth of the matter would seem to be that, while he has loosened himself from the bonds of earlier moral standards and beliefs, he has not replaced these guides for conduct with any other set of principles. The autonomous conscience of Puritanism has been replaced by the "radar-directed" conduct of the "marketer." [40] He tends to take his judgments as to what is right and wrong, proper and improper, from the changing culture as it impinges on him through the various social institutions and media of communication. This makes for a certain flexibility in attitudes toward other cultures and ideologies. But the flexibility is negative rather than positive. That is, the American has moved away from older moral and traditional norms without acquiring new bases of judgment. His toleration of difference therefore is unstable, and there is a substratum of ideological fundamentalism which frequently breaks through the surface and has an important impact on foreign policy. Thus in our efforts to stabilize the weakened and chaotic areas of Western Europe we have been prepared to go a long way in aiding "Socialist Great Britain" and the left-inclined powers of Western Europe. But there is a continual sabotage of this tolerance, frequent efforts at ideological imperialism, even occasional interferences at the administrative level, which are motivated by ideological fundamentalism.

In general, this intolerance of difference is more clearly expressed in periods of normalcy. Thus, even though the possibility appears to be remote, the prospect of a recrudescence of isolationism cannot be excluded. A tactical cessation of Russian pressure might produce just this kind of demobilization and withdrawal reaction and the reassertion of older principles of conduct. This is not to say that such a reaction would be decisive so far as policy is concerned; but it is a prospect which sound policy-planning should anticipate.

5. Idealism-Cynicism

In still another respect American moral predispositions may have consequences for foreign policy. The annoyance and irritation of the peoples of foreign countries over American self-righteousness is, on the whole, a relatively minor source of difficulty. Americans would appear to be happiest when they can cloak an action motivated by self-interest with an aura of New Testament selflessness, when an action which is "good business," or "good security" can be made to "look good" too. Similarly there is resistance among Americans over the straightforward expression of conscience-motivated behavior. What is "good" has to be represented as satisfying the criteria of self-interest. They are happiest when they can allay the Christian conscience at the same time that they satisfy self-interested criteria. In this regard the peoples of foreign countries are well protected, perhaps overprotected, by their own cynicism.

But there are a number of respects in which this moral dualism may produce more serious problems for the policy-maker. There would appear to be a certain cyclical trend in American moral attitudes. The great wave of idealism in the first world war gave way to the cynicism about foreign countries of the 1920's. The friendliness for our British and French allies of World War I gave way to bitterness over their defaults on their indebtedness. A little more than a decade ago the little country of Finland had a place at the very center of the American heart because she had kept up her payments on her war debts, while the European powers which had defaulted, and on the fate of which our security rested, were prevented from borrowing money in the American capital market. The chiliastic faith in the reasonableness of the Russians has now been supplanted by deep resentment over their base ingratitude.

American generosity and humanitarianism is a tentative phenomenon. Along with impulses toward good will and generosity, there is a deep-seated suspicion that smart people don't act that way, that "only suckers are a soft touch." In this connection a recent study which appeared in a popular magazine is of considerable interest.[41] This investigation, claiming to have been based on "reliable sampling procedures," reflected a degree of religious piety among Americans considerably greater than had previously been estimated. Of greatest interest was its description of American attitudes toward ethics. It would appear that almost half of the sample was sharply aware of the conflict between what was "right" and the demands of secular life. A somewhat smaller proportion considered that religion influenced their activities in business, political and social life. Considerably more than half felt that their conduct toward neighbors was governed by the golden rule; but more than 80 per cent felt that their neighbors fell considerably short of the golden rule in their conduct toward their fellowmen.

Quite aside from the question of the full reliability of a study asking such "loaded" and personal questions, there seems to be confirmation here for the proposition regarding the moral dualism in the American character. The aspiration to conform to Christian ethical ideals is clearly present among most members of the culture, but there would appear to be a strong apprehension that such standards of conduct are inapplicable because the outside world does not behave that way. Hence any impulse toward ethically motivated generosity is impaired not only by the feeling that it will go unrequited, but that one's neighbors will ridicule it or attribute it to some concealed, self-interested motive.

It would appear to be a reasonable speculation from the foregoing findings that any action involving the giving or loaning of American wealth to foreign peoples, even though it be motivated by calculations of self-interest, activates this fear that "only a sucker is a soft touch." Under conditions of threat, such as those of the present, these doubts and suspicions about "giving things away" have been kept within manageable proportions. But in a period of temporary stabilization when the superficial aspect of the foreign situation encourages withdrawal reactions, these feelings may play a role of some significance.

6. Superiority-Inferiority

In a sense America is a nation of parvenus. A historically unique rate of immigration, social, and geographic mobility has produced a people which has not had an opportunity to "set," to acquire the security and stability which come from familiar ties, associations, rights, and obligations. It is per-

haps not accidental that in the vulgarization of psychoan-
alytic hypotheses in America in the last decades one of the
first to acquire popular currency was the "superiority-
inferiority" complex. In more stably stratified societies the
individual tends to have a greater sense of "location," a
broader and deeper identification with his social surround-
ings. He has not *made* his own identity, while in America a
large proportion of each generation is *self-made*. Being self-
made produces a certain buoyancy, a sense of mastery, but
it leaves the individual somewhat doubtful as to his social
legitimacy. This sense of insecurity and uncertainty may add
a strident note to American claims for recognition. This
may explain the stereotype of the American abroad, confronted with complex and ancient cultures, taking alcoholic
refuge in assertions of American moral, political, and technical virtue. It may also account for a feeling in the United
States that American diplomats are no match for the wiliness
and cunning of Old World negotiators. In other words,
Americans typically overreact in their self-evaluations. They
over- and under-estimate their skills and virtues, just as
they over- and under-estimate the skills and virtues of
other cultures and nations.

It is perhaps this quality among Americans—and among
the American elites—which strongly militates against a balanced and empathic appreciation of cultural and national
differences so essential to the development of an effective
diplomacy. One may entertain the hypothesis that Americans tend to judge other nations and cultures according to a
strictly American scoreboard, on the basis of which America
is bound to win. It is difficult for Americans to accept a humane conception of cultural and national differences. Somehow, other cultural values must be transmuted into an
American currency so that it becomes possible in a competi-

tion of national cultures to rate the United States as the "best all-around culture of the year."

There is a noticeable sensitivity among Americans on the score of cultural and intellectual inferiority. Only recently the American press cited the throngs of visitors to art museums exhibiting the Habsburg collection of paintings as effectively refuting European claims of American cultural inferiority. Feelings of crudeness and inferiority are not only expressed in the form of direct refutation by citing such evidence as the above; they also are frequently expressed in the tendency to equate esthetic and intellectual subtlety with lack of manliness—artists and intellectuals are "queers."

This superiority-inferiority ambivalence may manifest itself in policy-making in a number of ways. It may take the direct and perhaps more typical form of cultural arrogance —assertions of the superiority of the American way in politics, in economics, in social relations, in morality, or in the physical amenities of life. In this case the psychological mechanism involved is a reaction-formation; unconscious feelings of inferiority lead to the assertion of superiority. Or it may take the form of an admission of inferiority and an attribution of superiority to other cultures or elite groups. In either case there is an alienation from the real character and potentialities of the self. One either becomes an ideal and non-existent American—a *persona* American—or one rejects one's Americanism entirely and attempts to "pass," for example, into English or French culture. These formulations, of course, state the problem in the extreme for purposes of clarity.

These reactions have a selective appeal among the various elite groups. Thus American artists, writers, and intellectuals have historically tended to manifest inferiority feelings in the form of imitativeness, or in expatriation. It has been asserted that members of the American foreign service have tended to assimilate themselves too readily to foreign cultures and aristocratic "sets," perhaps at the expense of their American perspective. The tendency for American families of wealth and prestige to ape the English and Continental aristocracies is too well known to call for detailed comment. All of these groups have in common the quality of having differentiated themselves from the American pattern through extraordinary wealth, through artistic or intellectual deviation, or through long residence abroad. The more "representative" American—the Congressman for example—tends to manifest the simpler form of cultural arrogance.

Either inferiority or superiority feelings in relation to other cultures may have a negative effect on the national interest. Cultural arrogance may alienate other peoples, impair confidence in the United States among actual and potential allies, or aid in some measure in the mobilization of hostile sentiment among neutrals and potential enemies. Cultural subservience, particularly if manifested by American diplomats and negotiators, may result in real and unnecessary sacrifices of the national interest.

The hypothesis may also be advanced that there is a certain periodicity of national moods of confidence and lack of confidence. These have perhaps been associated in the United States with the fluctuations of the business cycle. One may speculate that not least among the catastrophic foreign policy consequences of a serious depression in the United States would be an impairment of national self-confidence, a sudden welling to the surface of underlying doubt, which might result in a weakening of foreign policy resolution, a feeling of being overextended, a need for contraction, for consolidation, for withdrawal.

Conclusion: The Many Faces of America

It would be unfortunate if the preceding analysis conveyed the impression of a neat periodicity of American foreign policy moods. Actually the American approach to foreign policy problems at any given time is a historically unique phenomenon. It is influenced not only by these (and other) ambivalences in the American character, but by the immediate historical background and the specific content of the foreign policy problem. While it is useful analytically to talk about the alternation of "normalcy" and "crisis" moods, it must be recognized that crises differ from one another, just as do periods of normalcy, and that the American character is undergoing continual change. Thus from one era to the next, both the subjective and objective components of foreign policy moods may greatly change.

In the period before World War II, the dominant and overt foreign policy mood was a composite of withdrawal impulses, cynicism about power politics, intolerance of foreign peoples and cultures, and pessimism about the prospects of idealistic internationalism. Many experiences had combined to produce this state of mind. The development of a power structure in Europe which did not immediately and overtly threaten the United States provided a plausible justification for isolationism. Disillusionment over the collapse of the high moral purposes of the Allies in World War I provoked a cynical and pessimistic reaction which strengthened the withdrawal trend. The default on Allied war debts contributed to American arrogance with regard to the inefficiency and lack of integrity of foreign governments.

The growing threat to American security began to undermine this withdrawal mood in the late 1930's. But it took

the catastrophe of Pearl Harbor to produce a broad interventionist consensus. American intolerance of foreign countries and social systems was supplanted by a tolerance of
actual and potential allies. Cynicism and pessimism about international power politics were supplanted by moderately
idealistic aspirations and somewhat optimistic expectations
of peace and international amity.

This mood pattern lasted through the latter years of the
war and the brief period of Allied amity which followed
it. But as specific conflicts with the Soviet Union broadened
into the general impasse of the Cold War, the American
foreign policy mood changed again. Optimism about the
future of peace gave way to pessimism. Idealist internationalism faded into "security realism." Overtones of impatience
and intolerance began to emerge in public reactions to our
relations with the Soviet Union, England, China; but the
continuance of threat precluded an unequivocal expression
of these reactions.

There is some value for the purposes of foreign policy
planning in recognizing that an overtly interventionist and
"responsible" United States hides a covertly isolationist
longing, that an overtly tolerant America is at the same
time barely stifling intolerance reactions, that an idealistic
America is muttering *sotto voce* cynicisms, that a surface
optimism in America conceals a dread of the future. Understanding of these ambivalences might save statesmen periodic shocks at the sequences of American moods. One must
always take into account the fact that Americans in this
period of their development are both responsible and irre-
sponsible. A momentary rift in the clouds brings the irre-
sponsible trends to the surface; an intensification of threat
brings out a sober readiness to sacrifice.

America's contemporary role in world politics is hardly

more than a decade old. Other nations have had generations to assimilate their great political lessons. That America has begun to assimilate some of its political lessons is suggested by the widespread resolution that it can no longer tolerate the degree of economic instability which has characterized the past. This rejection of the inevitability of the severe shocks of the business cycle is matched in the political sphere by a growing acceptance of our foreign policy status and the sacrifices it imposes. But with regard to the foreign policy cycle, as well as the business cycle, a confident sense of self-mastery is still lacking.

Another impression which analysis of American moods may have conveyed is that these reactions are equally distributed among the entire population. We shall have the occasion to observe at a later point that there are substantially different mood susceptibilities at different points in the social and political structure. Social classes, age groups, men and women, and the various educational levels approach foreign policy problems from different emotional and intellectual starting points. The fact that there are so many different Americas is not only attributable to attitude instability *through time,* but also to the fact that *at any given time* there is a bewildering variety of moods and foreign policy proposals.

Within the framework of these general hypotheses the tasks of the three chapters which follow are to describe recent movements of foreign policy opinion among the American people, and to locate special susceptibilities within the social and political structure.

IV. The Instability of Mood

THE reaction of the general population to foreign policy issues has been described as one of mood. This is to say that foreign policy attitudes among most Americans lack intellectual structure and factual content. Such superficial psychic states are bound to be unstable since they are not anchored in a set of explicit value and means calculations or traditional compulsions. A second hypothesis which has been proposed is that this mass approach to foreign policy problems is a consequence of the extraordinary absorption of most Americans with the values of private material welfare.

There is little doubt that these same observations could be made about the peoples of foreign countries. But from two points of view, these popular tendencies in the United States have an especially significant impact on the making of foreign policy. In most Western European countries there is a well-established tradition of involvement in foreign affairs. While the masses may be quite uninformed and uninterested in specific foreign policy questions, there is a general readiness to accept foreign policy risks and commitments. In the United States such a tradition may be in the making, but it is clear that there is a great resistance to the acceptance of permanent involvement and a nostalgia for the earlier age of foreign policy innocence. Consequently, American "privatism" has greater significance for policy-making than, for example, similar tendencies among the English.

Secondly, the "popular mentality" has a greater influence

on policy in the United States than in many other countries. A greater decentralization of power and a greater political and social mobility constantly renew the political elites in the United States, bringing fresh and often blank minds to roles of public influence and foreign policy responsibility. In other countries the rate of political mobility is slower, and a stronger tradition of professionalism gives a wider scope to the foreign policy expert.

In addition to this pull of privatism, the very complexity of foreign affairs and the infinitesimal share of influence over the developments of world politics which the average American can realistically claim have the effect of discouraging interest and participation and providing justifications for indifference and lack of information. It would be an error to treat this tendency as a simple matter of "pathology," as many students of this problem suggest. It also has a "healthy" aspect, a readiness to accept a political division of labor which seems somehow to be more suited to the complexity of modern life than the older ideal of an alert yeomanry. Along with this acceptance of passivity there has developed a readiness to be guided by "professionals." Most Americans reserve the right to be skeptical and even cynical about the advice of their policy experts. But our demands for popular control appear to be satisfied as long as there are competing groups of experts and as long as the ultimate electoral power is reserved to the rank and file.

Foreign Affairs in the Focus of Attention

Under normal circumstances the American public has tended to be indifferent to questions of foreign policy because of their remoteness from everyday interests and activities. When foreign policy questions assume the aspect of immediate threat to the normal conduct of affairs they break into the focus of attention and share the public consciousness with private and domestic concerns.[1] It is not the foreign or domestic character of the issue which determines the accessibility of public attention, but the intimacy of the impact. From this point of view, foreign policy, save in moments of grave crisis, has to labor under a handicap; it has to shout loudly to be heard even a little.

One of the most interesting accumulations of evidence on this general question of the focus of public attention is a series of Gallup Polls which has been conducted since 1935.[2] On more than twenty occasions during this fifteen year period the American Institute of Public Opinion has asked a sample of the public: "What do you regard as the most important problem before the American people today?" The wording has been changed from time to time but not in such ways as to impair its value as a crude indication of the prominence of different types of issues in the public mind. The form of the question has the advantage of registering spontaneous responses. In the multiple choice or "yes-no" type of question one can never be sure that the respondent draws a clear distinction between what is really on his mind and what he thinks ought to be on his mind. The undirected response is a more reliable indication of the real degree and extent of spontaneous interest in foreign policy problems. In still another respect this type of question produces useful insights. It not only tells us about the comparative salience of foreign and domestic issues, but it permits the respondents to formulate the issues. Thus we can get an idea of the form in which the issue occurs in the focus of attention or the particular aspect of the problem which has acquired prominence.

Among the findings of this series of polls two call for

special comment: (1) the extreme dependence of public interest in foreign affairs on dramatic and overtly threatening events; (2) the extraordinary pull of domestic and private affairs even in periods of international crisis.

In the fall and winter of 1935 (see Table I), after the conclusion of the Italo-Abyssinian War and before the outbreak of the Spanish Civil War, 11 per cent of the Gallup sample selected international questions as the most vital before the American people. Almost all of those who stressed foreign policy formulated the issue as "maintaining American neutrality." The dominant questions troubling Americans had to do with employment, government economy, the depression, taxation, and the like. The main interest in foreign policy was negative. It was concerned with the avoidance of foreign involvement. By December of 1936, during the Spanish Civil War, the percentage of those who were especially apprehensive about threats from abroad and concerned with the maintenance of American neutrality had risen to 26 per cent. In December of 1937 the percentage was approximately the same as in the previous year, but attention had focused on the Far East in conjunction with the intensification of the Sino-Japanese War and the sinking of the American gunboat *Panay* by the Japanese.

The next Gallup "sounding" was made in January, 1939, after the surrender of the Spanish Loyalists and the conclusion of the Munich Pact. During this period of overt calm in international politics, foreign policy interest as measured by this index stood at 14 per cent. Eleven per cent thought that the preservation of peace was the most important issue before the American public; 3 per cent were concerned with the national defense. The violation of the Munich Pact through the occupation of Bohemia and Moravia and the Italian invasion of Albania resulted in a sudden shift in the

TABLE I

PERCENTAGE WHO REGARDED FOREIGN POLICY ISSUES
AS THE MOST IMPORTANT PROBLEMS FACING THE
AMERICAN PEOPLE *

Date	% Naming Foreign Problems as Most Vital
Nov. 1935	11
Dec. 1936	26
Dec. 1937	23
Jan. 1939	14
Apr. 1939	35
Dec. 1939	47
Aug. 1940	48
Nov. 1941	81
. . . †	
Oct. 1945	7
Feb. 1946	23
June 1946	11
Sep. 1946	23
Dec. 1946	22
Mar. 1947	54
July 1947	47
Sep. 1947	28
Dec. 1947	30
Feb. 1948	33
Apr. 1948	73
June 1948	50
Oct. 1949	34

* This material is adapted from polls taken by the American Institute of Public Opinion.

† Polls taken during the wartime period were omitted because they differed significantly in wording from the pre-war and postwar questions.

focus of attention in the spring of 1939. Thirty-five per cent were now aware of the foreign crisis and defined the most important issue facing the American people as "keeping out of war."

Unfortunately no poll was taken at the time of the Nazi-

Soviet pact and the outbreak of World War II. It is probable that these developments resulted in a dramatic rise in awareness of the international situation. By December of 1939, when the question was again included in the Gallup ballot, the "phoney war" period had probably caused a decline in interest. The proportion of those most concerned about foreign affairs was 47 per cent. The dominant foreign affairs issue was still defined as "keeping out of war." Nine months later after the fall of Norway, Denmark, France, and the Low Countries the figure was at 48 per cent. But by this time the issue was formulated in different terms. Only 9 per cent listed "keeping out of war" as the most important American problem. Twenty-seven per cent were now concerned with the adequacy of national defense. Twelve per cent spoke of the "war problem." Hitler's conquests of the spring and summer of 1940 had shaken confidence in our capacity to remain aloof from the international crisis. The approach to foreign policy was no longer one of simple rejection and withdrawal. The threat of German, Italian, and Japanese aggression had permeated the American consciousness to the point where tentative but positive steps were being supported.

By November of 1941—the eve of Pearl Harbor—public anxiety about the trend of international affairs had reached a point at which the vast majority of Gallup respondents listed issues related to foreign policy and national defense as the most important. In early November, 1941, 70 per cent listed such issues as the most vital. In late November, 81 per cent took this position. The problem was defined at this time as one of strengthening national defense as swiftly as possible, extending aid to Great Britain, and entering the European War. Only a small percentage still defined the issue as "keeping us out of war" (7 per cent in early November, 9 per cent in late November).

The polls taken on this question during the course of World War II have to be considered separately since the question was formulated differently. The respondents were asked, *"Aside from winning the war,* what do you think is the most important problem facing this country today?" There is little doubt that repetition of the earlier wording would have produced figures even higher than those recorded in November, 1941. As it is, the wartime version of the question produced highly suggestive results. Only small percentages of the three wartime samples considered foreign policy problems (aside from winning the war) as the most vital. In December, 1942, 11 per cent were concerned with "making a lasting peace," and 8 per cent were troubled about the problem of postwar reconstruction. The great majority listed inflation, the danger of depression, the food shortage, and the labor problem as the vital issues before the country. It is of special interest that the percentage of those naming foreign policy issues (aside from winning the war) as the most important *declined* rather than increased as the successful conclusion of the war became more imminent. Thus in August, 1943, only 14 per cent listed foreign policy questions; in March, 1945, on the eve of the German collapse, the same proportion listed such questions; and immediately after V-J Day (late August, 1945) only 6 per cent were acutely concerned with international problems.

What these figures suggest is that there was relatively little interest during the war period in the problems of the postwar settlement and postwar security, as compared with questions which appeared as more urgent, such as postwar conversion, employment, and the like. Other polls taken at this time suggest, however, that the older pattern of American isolationism had largely disappeared. When confronted with the question as to whether the United States ought to play a larger part in world affairs than was the case in the past, very large majorities (between 70 and 80 per cent) were in favor of increased participation and only a small number continued to be isolationists in principle. Nevertheless, when not confronted with emotionally loaded questions, only small percentages during the height of the war placed long-run problems of international relations at the center of their attention.

These findings suggest that the American attitude toward involvement in foreign affairs is a more complex and elusive phenomenon than is ordinarily supposed. It cannot be understood in its own terms but has to be seen in the light of the general American value orientation. The average American is so deeply and tensely involved with immediate, private concerns that any diversion of attention meets with powerful resistance. When political issues impinge, or threaten to impinge, upon these concerns, public attention broadens to include them. But the moment the pressure is reduced there is a swift withdrawal, like the snapping back of a strained elastic. The will to participate in world affairs is an intellectual and learned attitude validated by immediate experience and moral pressure. But the acceptance of the implications of America's position in world affairs comes with great reluctance, and it may only be possible to motivate it in response to obvious and overt threats.

The changes in the focus of attention since the end of World War II illustrate the persistence of this unstable and superficial response to problems of world politics.

In late August of 1945 American interest in foreign affairs collapsed. The public recognized intellectually that the change in the power position of the United States meant that the familiar pattern of isolationism could not be reasserted. But as a serious problem calling for thought and information—as a stable primary interest—problems of foreign affairs concerned a very small minority of Americans. Six per cent in August, 1945, and 7 per cent in October, 1945, listed "keeping the peace," "European rehabilitation," and "controlling the atomic bomb" as matters of first concern before the American people.

Subsequent movements of opinion demonstrate two points. First, there has been an increasing secular trend of interest in foreign affairs as the East-West conflict has intensified. But, secondly, the responses continue to be highly unstable, suddenly rising in relation to immediate threat and suddenly collapsing in relation to superficial and temporary stabilizations in U.S.-U.S.S.R. tensions. Thus, in early 1946 there was a sudden increase in interest as a consequence of the Iranian crisis. Six months later, progress with the Satellite and Italian peace treaties resulted in a sharp decline in public attention. In the fall of 1946 the Wallace-Byrnes controversy brought about a sharpened interest in problems of foreign policy. The announcement of the Truman Doctrine in the spring of 1947 produced a sharp rise to a postwar peak of 54 per cent. But again, the announcement of the Marshall Plan, the enactment of the "Interim Aid Bill," and the defeat of the Cominform-initiated strikes in France during the summer and fall of 1947 apparently produced an atmosphere of safety. A Gallup question in December, 1947, showed a drop of some 20 per cent in those viewing foreign issues as the most important.

The Italian electoral crisis of April, 1948, produced another sudden rise in public attention, only to be followed by a decline in the period immediately after the victory of the non-Communist parties. The superficial and threat-bound character of the American attitudes toward international affairs is clearly indicated by these sudden and dramatic shifts in attention. It should however be pointed out that since the onset of the Cold War substantial percentages of national samples have consistently placed the highest priority on foreign policy issues. Thus in the late spring of 1948, before the imposition of the Soviet blockade on Berlin, a comparatively "non-crisis" period, 50 per cent of those interviewed listed "foreign policy" and related questions as the "most important problems facing this country today." In the early fall of 1949, before the announcement of the atomic explosion in the Soviet Union, 34 per cent listed foreign policy problems as the most important.

It can hardly be argued on the basis of available evidence that the decline of intense interest in foreign affairs immediately after the end of World War II was comparable to the wave of isolationism which swept the United States after the first world war. Other questions asked during the late period of World War II and the year immediately following the war show that a considerable part of the public was ready to give some priority (if not first priority) to American participation in foreign affairs. A *Fortune* poll released on December 29, 1944, listed a number of issues before the United States and asked the respondents to check which items they considered to be most important. Almost sixty per cent listed "The part the U.S. should play in world affairs after the war."

While it can be said, therefore, that questions of foreign affairs were recognized to be of importance, other studies suggest a tendency to push troublesome and remote questions aside. Thus a *Fortune* poll released in August, 1945, showed that more than half of the sample felt that Russia and the problems of the defeated countries would be "troublesome problems in the next few years." A later Gallup question showed how misleading it would have been to conclude that large numbers of Americans actually gave much thought to our relations with Russia. Gallup, in a poll conducted at the end of September, 1946, divided his sample into two equal parts and asked the respondents to select from a list of issues the problems which interested them most. Only 15 per cent of the first half of the sample were *most* interested in the problem of "dealing with Russia"; 14 per cent were "second most interested." In the second half of the sample the foreign affairs question was phrased "keeping peace in the world." Sixty-three per cent picked this problem as the one in which they were most interested.

These two polls suggest some interesting hypotheses about American attitudes toward the Russian problem and foreign affairs. When a sample of American respondents is offered a "gift package" like "keeping peace in the world," they express an enormous interest in foreign affairs. They are interested if the issue is formulated in simplified, panacean terms. They are also ready to recognize that problems of foreign affairs—such as our relations with Russia—are important and troublesome problems. But if you ask them whether dealing with Russia—that most difficult and most serious foreign affairs problem—interests them most, and place this alternative among such issues as the housing problem, reducing the cost of living, strikes, and the like, the percentage drops to an extremely small minority.

American interest in foreign affairs thus continues to have impatient and strong negative overtones. Americans recognize that they are involved in foreign politics and cannot fully indulge their impulses toward withdrawal. But when confronted by the real tedium, tension, threat, and frustration of our relations with Russia they show an unwillingness to involve and interest themselves. On the positive side it should be recognized that there is some evidence of a growing resolution to maintain a high and stable level of interest in foreign affairs. This is especially evident in more recent surveys. A *Fortune* poll released in June, 1948, asked: "Suppose that only four of these things could be handled in the way you think right in the next four years. Which would you select as most important?" Of the four answers with largest percentages, three referred to foreign policy problems. Sixty-nine per cent listed "our military strength," 66 per cent listed "our policy toward Russia," and 53 per cent cited "the Marshall Plan." In an intensive study of attitudes toward foreign affairs in the community of Cincinnati, the National Opinion Research Center asked its respondents whether they take a "keen, mild, or practically no interest" in news about domestic and foreign issues.[3] Ninety-two per cent were keenly interested in news about the cost of living, 54 per cent in our relations with Russia, and 51 per cent in the control of the atomic bomb. There can be little question that awareness of foreign policy problems at the present time is high. But the previous record of fluctuations suggests the possibility of a future decline of interest under less overtly threatening conditions.

Information About Foreign Affairs

The superficiality of the involvement of most Americans with problems of world politics is also suggested by the extremely limited character of the information about international affairs which most of them have. The extent of this information is perhaps a better index of effective interest in world problems than direct questions about the degree of that interest. If interest in our relations with Russia, the

Marshall Plan, or the control of atomic energy were "keen," one might expect some familiarity with the details of these problems. When an average American is keenly interested in a problem such as the next season's prospects of the major league ball clubs he often displays considerable erudition and analytical virtuosity. Only a minute proportion of them bring such learning and skill to bear on problems of foreign policy. This is not to suggest that Americans are different from other peoples in this regard. Polling evidence from foreign countries testing information on foreign affairs shows just about the same results. But in the absence of a well-established tradition of participation in foreign affairs a lack of information on foreign policy problems among the American people may affect policy more significantly in the United States than it would in foreign countries.

The surveys which have been made of the level of information on foreign affairs in the United States show that most Americans have a quite casual and external acquaintance with the facts of world affairs. A survey made in 1946 classified a sample of the population into seven information groups ranging from high to low. The schedule tested knowledge of the most elementary kind. Respondents were classified in group one if they (1) knew the name of the current Secretary of State, (2) could identify General Leslie R. Groves, (3) name the country then being charged with keeping troops in Iran longer than she was supposed to, (4) could name a material from which atomic energy was being derived, (5) knew of the plan to test the atomic bomb in the near future, and (6) could identify the targets on which the bomb was to be tested. At the time of the survey all of these items were being prominently mentioned in the newspapers. Sixteen per cent were unable to identify any of these items. Eight per cent could identify all of them. Sixty-two per cent fell into the category of knowing three or fewer of the six items.[4]

In the Cincinnati study which was held in September, 1947, it was found that 30 per cent of the adult population were unfamiliar with the purposes of the United Nations. A nation-wide survey conducted a few months before showed that 36 per cent of a national sample were similarly uninformed. Of the 70 per cent in the Cincinnati sample who were aware of the general purpose of the United Nations a considerable proportion were confused as to its scope of action. Thus 55 out of 70 per cent thought that the United Nations, among its other functions, was supposed to work out the peace treaties with Germany and Japan.[5]

Martin Kriesberg in his study of American information on foreign affairs estimated that about thirty per cent of the electorate, on the average, are "unaware of almost any given event in American foreign policy." Forty-five per cent are "aware but uninformed." These people retain little information. Although they may follow discussions of the issues of foreign policy, they "cannot frame intelligent arguments about them." He estimates at twenty-five per cent the proportion who show "knowledge of foreign problems." [6]

According to survey findings only an extremely small proportion of the public belong to organizations in which foreign affairs are sometimes discussed. The National Opinion Research Center in November, 1947, found only some 16 per cent who were members of clubs, societies, or trade-unions in which such issues were occasionally talked about. The Survey Research Center in February, 1947, reported only 10 per cent of its sample in this category. The latter survey also found a high correlation between membership in such organizations and level of information in foreign affairs. It also found that participation in organizations occasionally discussing foreign affairs was linked with high income and education. Thus 24 per cent of those having annual incomes of $5000 or more, and 30 per cent of those who had completed a college education were officers or members of such organizations. In the Cincinnati study the part of the sample (85 per cent) which was not affiliated with organizations of this kind was queried, "Is there any particular reason why you don't?" Forty-two per cent "didn't know why"; 23 per cent were "too busy"; most of the remainder offered a variety of specific reasons all implying indifference.[7]

As has already been suggested, it would be a one-sided interpretation of American interest in foreign policy problems if we were only to stress the pressure of private concerns and the persistence of traditional attitudes. If these factors have the effect of pulling people away from the foreign policy arena, the very complexity of world politics and the minute and indirect share of influence which the average person can exercise in this field have the effect of repelling interest and involvement. Most Americans either feel that they can do nothing about improving the world situation, or are ignorant of what they can do. Those who think that they can do something suggest types of action (such as obeying the Ten Commandments, or electing good men to office) which are not clear and compelling directives to acquire information on foreign affairs.[8] In this connection perhaps the "man in the street" is sounder than some of the public opinion experts. Even if he were to meet the standards set by the polling experts, he would hardly be better off in evaluating foreign policy proposals than he is in his present state of ignorance. Some of the public opinion experts appear to operate on the theory that with each increment of knowledge there is an increment of increased capacity to understand foreign policy problems. In actual fact it takes many, many increments of knowledge plus much wisdom before a body of factual data takes on meaningful proportions and can lead to intelligent criticism of foreign policy. So-called public apathy and indifference are at least in part an acceptance of a sound division of labor in a complex and interdependent world.

Interest in foreign affairs, information about foreign affairs, and the sense of being able to play an active and meaningful role in the arena of political decision appear to go hand in hand. These characteristics appear to be concentrated among the more well-to-do and better educated elements of the population (see Chapter VI). Thus the opinion elites which are largely recruited from this more alert stratum of the population undoubtedly constitute a more stable and deeply involved group in relation to foreign affairs. If the policy and opinion elites constitute the source of foreign policy proposals and the point at which debate on the merits of these proposals takes place, then the educated and more well-to-do stratum of the population is that part of the mass audience which is attentive to this debate.

From Isolation to Participation

Despite this passivity and indifference to the facts and details of world affairs the evidence suggests that the older conception of isolationism no longer has large and powerful support among the American people. From the beginning of the war until the present time all of the polls show large majorities ready to accept a general policy of active involvement.[9] Other studies have shown a substantial readiness to set aside traditional views and to make personal sacrifices to maintain this active world role.[10]

Thus the rigidity of isolationism has been replaced by a newer plasticity. But this readiness to support an active world role has to be qualified in a number of ways. The undertow of withdrawal is still very powerful. Deeply ingrained traditions do not die easy deaths. The world outside is still remote for most Americans; and the tragic lessons of the last decades have not been fully digested. Readiness to participate and to sacrifice appear to be unstable and threat-bound. They are based not on a mature fear of the consequences of irresponsibility, but more on immediate anxieties which rise and subside with fluctuations in international tension.

The implications of this general orientation toward foreign policy are of considerable significance. The superficiality and instability of public concern places enormous power in the hands of the policy and opinion elites. There is no corrective available in matters calling for immediate action if serious miscalculations are made at the elite level. The triumph of Communism in China is a case in point. Here not only was the public uninformed and inadequately motivated, but among the policy and opinion elites only a shallow and perfunctory discussion of these urgent issues took place. For a foreign policy which is democratic, in the sense in which that is possible, the discussion of issues must have depth. The various public and private elite groups must participate on the basis of familiarity with the issues. If only a handful of experts are informed and concerned and there is no real policy competition before the "attentive public," there is a grave danger that the merits of a problem will not receive adequate attention and that accidental elite biases will obscure significant security interests. This problem is to be discussed in greater detail at another point. Here it is only necessary to point out that the role of elites is of special importance in the field of foreign policy.

The instability of moods and the typical public indifference to foreign policy in the absence of threat accords a disproportionate influence to minority groups. American policy toward Palestine is a case in point. The pressure of economy-minded conservatives, the high tariff interests and the anti-military-training groups are other illustrations of the power of relatively small but powerful interests. Finally, the superficiality and instability of public attitudes toward foreign affairs creates the danger of under and over-reaction to changes in the world political situation. This unstable atmosphere surrounding our foreign policy makes anything better than a series of improvisations difficult to achieve. Effective policy-planning calls for decisions and actions taken in advance in order to cope with anticipated crises. There is a serious danger that the public mood necessary to support such action only develops in response to the crisis itself, and long after anticipatory and preventive action can be effectively taken.

V. Changes in the Foreign Policy Mood

THE comparative disinterest in problems of world politics in the period immediately following World War II was linked to a widespread, if moderate, optimism about the future of American foreign relations. The prospect of another war was placed in the remote future. There was substantial satisfaction with United States-Russian co-operation. There was some hope for the United Nations Organization. There was relatively little anxiety about the problem of American security.

In the four years following the end of the war this mood has changed in a number of ways. The impulse to withdraw to private interests and pursuits has given way to a reluctant awareness of the threat to American security. Optimism has been supplanted by pessimism, confidence in the future by anxiety. A moderate indulgence in disinterested charitableness and generosity has been supplanted by a readiness for sacrifices justified by security calculations. Disenchantment has taken the place of the pianissimo of idealism in the war years and the period immediately following. At the same time, the national mood is not one of panic or war fever. The mood is still plastic and relatively passive. It is ready to support policy initiatives within the general limits of firm action. If it does not foreclose negotiation in efforts at attaining national security, it also does not preclude actions that involve the risk of war. In the present period of threat this mood of passivity and plasticity lends itself to long-range policy-planning, although there is no guarantee that the public mood will continue to support such policies in the absence of a clear threat. The American foreign policy mood is permissive; it will follow the lead of the policy elites if they demonstrate unity and resolution. The decline of isolationism has widened the scope of discretion of the policy and opinion elites. The problem of contemporary American foreign policy is not so much one of mass traditions and resistances as it is one of resolution, courage, and intelligence of the leadership.

Thus, the findings reported here lend support to our hypotheses concerning the implications of the American character for foreign policy. In the last four years there has been a significant shift from withdrawal tendencies to interventionist tendencies, from optimistic expectations to pessimistic expectations, from moderate idealism to greater realism. In the face of crisis the immediate postwar mood has given way to resolution based on simplified conceptions of foreign policy problems. From the Truman Doctrine to Point Four our policies have been in part proposed and accepted with panacean overtones which have somewhat obscured the long, unrelenting, and unpredictable grind of foreign policy in the era of the cold war.

At the same time, these data will suggest that these cyclical shifts have been less extreme than in the past, that fluctuations in the opinion cycle may be leveling off, and that there is increasing recognition of the costs of indulging moods. And perhaps there is taking shape in the thinking and feeling of this youthful people of "yea-sayers" a more mature sense of the ever-present possibility of tragedy and frustration.

Popular Expectations of War

According to the available evidence most Americans do not believe in the likelihood of permanent peace. However, in June, 1943, a survey showed that more than 60 per cent of a national sample thought "the chances for making a lasting peace after this war will be . . . better than they were after the last war." [1] This, of course, did not represent a conviction, but the mere expression of an opinion that the prospects for peace were better. Less than two years later, when the United States was in the full flush of victory, only 45 per cent of a national sample were ready to say that the United States would not again be involved in a war within the succeeding twenty-five years. When this more optimistic part of the sample together with those who had expressed no opinion (a combined total of 62 per cent) were asked whether they thought the United States would find itself in a war within a fifty-year period, only 19 per cent persisted in the conviction that a peace of this duration was in prospect. [2] A month before V-J Day another polling organization [3] asked the same question and found that 42 per cent of a national sample thought we would again be involved in a war within a twenty-five year period; 19 per cent thought the war would not take place before twenty-five to thirty years; and 16 per cent refused to commit themselves. Only 23 per cent thought war could be postponed for more than fifty years.

It was clear in this period, however, that a relatively large number of people held the conviction that another war, while probable, was a matter of the more or less remote future. Secondly, although most Americans were reluctant to commit themselves fully on the prospects of long-range peace, they were ready to admit that there was a fairly good chance that it might be maintained over a long period of time.

A number of points may be made by way of characterization of this mood of optimism. While only a relatively small number believed that the millennium was at hand, most of us apparently felt that we were faced with a long period of peace. The comparatively large number who were convinced that we would be involved in another war within twenty-five years were hardly pessimists. They might be better described as curbstone philosophers of history. It did not cost anything to take a more skeptical view, since the psychological time-span was sufficiently long to justify the withdrawal of attention from problems of war and peace and world politics.

In Tables II, III, and IV the transformations of this

TABLE II

PERCENTAGE WHO EXPECT THE UNITED STATES TO BE AT WAR WITHIN THE NEXT TWENTY-FIVE YEARS *

Date	% Expecting War in 25 Years
Mar. 1945	38
Aug. 1945	40
Oct. 1945	54
Mar. 1946	64
May 1946	62
Sep. 1946	62
Mar. 1947	73
July 1947	73
Feb. 1948	76

* This material is adapted from polls taken by the American Institute of Public Opinion and the National Opinion Research Center.

originally optimistic view are traced from March, 1945, to early 1949. The proportion of those who thought the United

TABLE III

PERCENTAGE WHO EXPECT THE UNITED STATES TO
BE AT WAR WITHIN THE NEXT TEN YEARS *

Date	% Expecting War in 10 Years
Mar. 1946	49
Mar. 1947	50
July 1947	53
Oct. 1947	54
Feb. 1948	54
Mar. 1948	74

* This material is adapted from polls taken by the American Institute of Public Opinion and the National Opinion Research Center.

TABLE IV

PERCENTAGE WHO EXPECT THE UNITED STATES TO
BE AT WAR WITHIN THE NEXT YEAR *

Date	% Expecting War in One Year
Sep. 1946	3
Sep. 1948	32
Nov. 1948	21
May 1949	15

* This material is adapted from polls taken by the American Institute of Public Opinion.

States would again be involved in a war within twenty-five years increased from 38 per cent in early 1945 to 64 per cent in March, 1946, during the height of the Iranian crisis. Since this time the proportion convinced of the likelihood of war within twenty-five years has increased, reaching a high point around the time of the Czech crisis when 76 per cent expressed this opinion.

Of greater interest is the fact that the percentages expecting war within ten years and one year have risen sharply in the past three years. During the Iranian crisis almost half of a national sample thought war would occur within a ten year period. During the Czech crisis this figure jumped to 74 per cent.

Expectation of war within twenty-five years or ten years is hardly an indication of panic. Expectation of war within a year, however, is clear evidence of a feeling of immediate threat. While it might be said that some of those convinced of the likelihood of war within twenty-five years or even ten years were being modishly realistic or cynical, this could not be said of those who viewed war as a matter of months or at most a year. In September, 1946, only 3 per cent of a national sample expressed the opinion that war was likely within so short a time. In September, 1948, in conjunction with the Berlin crisis, something approximating a real war scare was evident. Thirty-two per cent viewed war as likely within the year. Another poll taken during the Berlin crisis showed that 80 per cent of a national sample were ready to stay in Berlin "even if it means war with Russia." [4]

The success of the airlift and the resolution of the Berlin crisis resulted in a decline in the percentage of those expecting war within a year to 15 per cent. But while this "war panic" has passed, the evidence suggests a definitely increasing pessimism about the prospects of peace. Well over a majority of respondents in all the polls taken on this subject claim that they expect a war within ten or fifteen years. Only a very small number feel that if we can manage to get over the immediate crises of the present, there will be a better prospect for long-run peace. [5]

Attitudes Toward Russia

The available quantitative evidence concerning American attitudes toward Russia may be treated under three headings: (1) appraisals of Russian aims and intentions, (2) expectations of Russian co-operation, and (3) appraisals of American policy toward Russia. Broadly speaking, a large proportion of the American public during the course of the war and a brief period subsequent to it viewed Soviet aims as unaggressive, thought the prospects for Russian-American co-operation were good, and thought that the United States ought to make a substantial effort to keep on good terms with Russia. A substantial part of those who did not take this view were noncommittal rather than unambiguously pessimistic.

This "honeymoon" atmosphere was a war phenomenon. During the period of the Nazi-Soviet pact more than a third of a national sample regarded Russia "as the worst influence in Europe." [6] Before the outbreak of the European war, evidence suggests that if they had to choose, more Americans would prefer fascism to communism.[7] About a third of a national sample (in June, 1937) would have preferred fascism as compared with 20 per cent favorable to communism. After the German invasion of Russia the proportion favoring fascism dropped to below 10 per cent, while more than 50 per cent would have preferred communism as a lesser evil.

Thus, while the distrust of Russia was strong in the prewar period, it was hardly a rigid hostility. A substratum of suspicion was persistent, but active hostility fluctuated with Russian actions. Consistent distrust was reflected in the prevailing substantial percentages of Americans who offered negative or noncommittal responses even during the period of the war. In January, 1942, 31 per cent of a national sample felt that Russia would turn against the democratic nations and try to overthrow their governments if she won the war against Germany.[8] The same organization found in

August, 1944, that 20 per cent of a national sample thought Russia would "take over a large part of Europe after the end of the war and try to spread Communism." Thirteen per cent expressed no opinion. Forty-five per cent felt Russia would not pursue an expansionist policy but would only attempt to attain security by ensuring the establishment of friendly governments on her borders. Another 22 per cent felt that Russia would follow "a real 'Good Neighbor' Policy."

Either confidence in Russian aims or a readiness to withhold judgment was the characteristic mood of the majority of the public at the end of the war. In January, 1945, almost seventy per cent thought that the United States would get along better with the Soviet Union in the postwar period than in the prewar period.[9] Another survey made at this time showed that according to informed American opinion, Russia, Great Britain, and the United States came off about equally well on the question of living up to the Atlantic Charter.[10] Nine months later, around the time of V-J Day, almost thirty per cent viewed Russian aims in Eastern Europe as "defensive"; about twenty-five per cent attached purely economic or humanitarian motives to Russia's Eastern European policy; 20 per cent had no opinion. Only 25 per cent thought Russia was trying to extend the Communist orbit in Eastern Europe.[11]

But this overtly favorable mood was troubled by some doubt and fear even among those who viewed Russia with moderate optimism. In response to a question asked in March, 1945, "What do you think the U.S. has most to fear from Russia after this war?" 29 per cent of a national sample showed concern with Communist ideology, Russian expansiveness and aggressiveness, and lack of good will.[12]

In general, one might crudely characterize the American

public in this period as being divided into three groups vis-à-vis Russia. First, there were those, perhaps twenty to thirty per cent, who were deeply and invariably distrustful. Second, a group of perhaps similar size was fully sold on Russia's amicable and peaceful intentions. Third, a broad middle group ranged from a noncommittal view to one of hope and moderate optimism. But even this middle group was troubled by some concern and doubt.

This mood of cautious optimism was soon dispelled. By July of 1946, a *Fortune* poll showed 50 per cent of a national sample thinking that Russia was out to dominate as much of the world as possible. Only 34 per cent thought that Russian policy was motivated by considerations of military security. Not much more than a year later the same polling organization recorded 66 per cent as viewing Russia as an aggressive nation "that would start a war to get something she wants." [13]

Independent opinion soundings by the Gallup organization confirm the trend described in the *Fortune* surveys. Since early 1946 well over a majority in a series of national samples viewed Russia as aiming "to build herself up to be the ruling power of the world." In February, 1948, 77 per cent had this view of Russian aims. Only 12 per cent viewed Russian policy as intended to maintain her security. This figure has to be understood in the light of the Czech crisis; but a subsequent sounding showed that well over two-thirds of a national sample continued to view Russian aims as aggressive.

These figures indicating American appraisals of Russian aims have to be taken with some caution. When American respondents are confronted with explicit appraisal of Russian aims, large majorities pick the most extreme formulation, "the ruling power of the world." In surveys relying on more spontaneous choices it would appear that most Americans have difficulty in believing that any country could have plans for world domination. Most Americans, on the basis of this type of survey, think of Russia as an aggressive power in somewhat vague terms. Only a third of the respondents in such a survey volunteered the opinion that Russian aims were without limits. Less than half felt that the United States was included in the Soviet program of domination. Most respondents were either undecided or attributed more limited objectives to the Soviet Union.[14]

Expectations of Russian co-operation in the postwar world have also become increasingly pessimistic. In late 1944 and early 1945 the great majority of Americans described themselves as satisfied with "Big Three" co-operation. Among those who were dissatisfied, Great Britain was far more frequently criticized than Russia. This situation changed with the exacerbation of the Polish crisis in the middle of 1945 when most of those dissatisfied with the progress of international co-operation blamed Russia for the deterioration.[15]

During the course of the war the percentage who thought Russia could be trusted to co-operate with us after hostilities ranged between 32 and 57 per cent. The "don't knows" averaged around twenty per cent. The percentage of those who thought Russia could not be trusted to co-operate ranged between 20 and 53 per cent. During 1946, the "distrustful" proportion exceeded 50 per cent on two occasions.[16] During the course of 1947 the proportion of those expecting co-operative behavior from Russians had declined from 33 to 16 per cent, while the proportion which did not count on such behavior had risen from 52 to 73 per cent.

In view of this rapid hardening of a generally negative attitude toward Soviet-Communist aims, it is hardly surprising that American sentiment has been ready to support an increasingly resolute policy with regard to Communist expansion. A series of *Fortune* and Gallup surveys in 1945, 1946, and 1947 reflect this hardening of attitude. In September, 1945, almost 23 per cent of a *Fortune* sample thought "we should make every possible effort" to keep on friendly terms with Russia. The wording of the question implied a readiness to "appease" Russia and a willingness to make concessions because of the overwhelming importance of Russian friendship. In a *Fortune* survey in July, 1946, this percentage dropped to 15 per cent; a Gallup repetition of the statement in June, 1947, elicited approval only from 6 per cent of the sample. During the same two-year period the proportion of those who considered Russian friendship as important, "but not so important that we should make too many concessions to her" remained stable at around fifty per cent. At the same time, those who urged a policy of having "as little as possible to do with Russia" had increased from 9 per cent in September, 1945, to 21 per cent in June, 1947.

Other studies suggest that by early 1946 the general public overwhelmingly favored a firm policy toward the Soviet Union. A series of Gallup surveys showed that 60 per cent or more of four national samples polled in 1946, 1947, and 1948 felt that American policy toward Russia was "too soft." Other sources suggest a little more concretely just how firm the American public wanted its policy to be. A *Fortune* survey released in January, 1947, found two-thirds of the sample agreeing to the proposition "Russia won't cooperate with us as long as we give in to her; the best way to get her to work with us for peace is to keep strong ourselves and make concessions only when we get something in return." Less than 25 per cent agreed that "Russia will cooperate with us to maintain peace if we try to understand her point of view and make some concessions in order to help solve her immediate problems."

In a question asked in March, 1948 (immediately following the Czech crisis), the respondents were given the opportunity to propose policies toward Russia without guidance from the interviewer. The sample was asked: "If Russia continues to follow her present course, what should we do, if anything?" Twenty-two per cent volunteered answers implying general firmness and no appeasement; 27 per cent suggested that we prepare to fight and build up our armed forces. Seventeen per cent suggested that we go to war. Another 6 per cent suggested more specific actions short of war. Only 9 per cent volunteered "appeasement" proposals. What is rather striking in this Czech crisis poll is that more than two-fifths of the sample spontaneously proposed war-preparatory action or war itself, while only a minute proportion spontaneously proposed negotiations or concessions.

If we take this poll in conjunction with one released two months later we get a rather impressive picture of the impatience and confusion pervading American attitudes toward Russia. In May, 1948, 63 per cent of a national sample "thought it would be a good idea . . . for President Truman to call an international meeting with Stalin and the heads of other nations to work out more effective plans for peace." [17] But only 24 per cent had confidence in the success of such a conference. A similar percentage, favoring the calling of such a conference, thought the conference would fail.

American opinion thus appears to be reaching a point of irritation and impatience at which action is being called for, whether this takes the form of strengthening the national defense, forming alliances, renewing negotiations in which the majority apparently have no confidence at all, or very little.

It would appear that the greater part of the American public since the spring of 1948 has been ready to back up American foreign policy with warlike measures if necessary. In late spring of 1948 a *Fortune* survey [18] found small majorities in favor of sending American military forces to France, Italy, Greece, or Turkey if it were necessary to prevent these countries from coming into the Russian orbit. Less than a third opposed such action; the remainders expressed no opinions. As we have already pointed out, 80 per cent of the sample in a Gallup poll (release date, July, 1948) were ready to back up our Berlin policy even if it meant war.

In brief summary it might be said that American sentiment, while not fixed on a war course toward Russia, is permissive of actions which involve the risk of war. The prospect of war with Russia is not a sufficient deterrent to dispel popular support of American policy in those areas in which we have assumed commitments. American sentiment does not preclude negotiations with the Russians in principle; but it has little confidence in their usefulness. At the same time this evidence should not be taken to imply a stable and resolute mood. It is a mood born of well-dramatized threat. It may again be pointed out that a tactical Russian withdrawal of pressure might quickly produce a subsidence of anxiety and resolution.

Attitudes Toward American Security

Along with an increasing sense of the imminence of war and deepening pessimism about the course of our relations with the Soviet Union, the public conception of American security policy has changed in a number of ways. There was some readiness to entrust American security to an international agency during the war and the immediate postwar period. Consistently, more than two-thirds of national samples approved American participation in an international organization after the war.[19] However, given the moral atmosphere of the period, such expressions of approval can be viewed as not a great deal more than general votes of confidence in virtue. In general, the campaign for the United Nations has contained religious overtones and has been led by the guardians of the community conscience—teachers, the clergy, and the various women's organizations.

When confronted with questions relating to the prospects of an international security organization, a substantial proportion registered some doubt about its future effectiveness. Thus in September, 1943, only 48 per cent thought that "a union of nations will have a . . . good . . . chance to prevent wars." Thirty-six per cent described the prospect as only fair, and 10 per cent thought it would have no chance at all.[20] In the spring of 1945 a national poll sounded out American opinion on its confidence in an international organization. Fifty-five per cent subscribed to the view that an international organization was really going to get started. Twenty-one per cent thought that an international organization would either be ineffective or would never be formed at all. Twenty-four per cent were "don't knows." [21]

Apparently skepticism as to the efficacy of international organization was even more widespread than these figures indicate. The general feeling in the United States was that international organization ought to be given its chance, and many individuals were ready to suppress their doubts in order to give it a good send-off. As soon as the question of future peace was separated from the emotionally loaded symbol of international organization, skepticism was more freely and generally expressed. Thus the National Opinion Research Center claimed that "Out of every four Americans, only one thinks that there is any chance at all of preventing

all wars after this one [World War II], and two think that
there will always be wars. The other one either thinks that
some day all wars will be prevented, or is undecided." [22]
At the same time, the great majority felt that the best way to
try to prevent wars was by means of international organization.

Perhaps the general background might be described as one
of benevolent skepticism, coupled with a general willingness to give international organization a try and to make
some sacrifices in order to make the trial a fair one. The
great mass of the public was not only skeptical, but somewhat indifferent to United Nations affairs. Sanguine expectations for, and genuine involvement with, the future of the
United Nations was characteristic of a militant and articulate
minority of educators, clergymen, community leaders, and
their followings.

Evidence as to the subsequent fate of American expectations for the future of the United Nations is of two types.
On the one hand, we have opinion surveys which directly
questioned people as to their satisfaction or dissatisfaction
with United Nations progress. On the other hand, we have
polls in which more spontaneous responses were made possible. The first type of evidence is contained in Table V.
During the entire course of the career of the United Nations
Organization the proportion of those "satisfied" with its
progress has never exceeded 39 per cent. The proportion
of "dissatisfied" has remained relatively stable at around
fifty per cent during 1947 and 1948. The "no opinion"
group has ranged from 30 to 16 per cent.

A vague question such as the above leaves largely unan-
swered the question as to the actual role played by the
United Nations in the security calculations of the American
public. More reliable indications are to be found in spontane-

TABLE V

APPRAISAL OF UNITED NATIONS PROGRESS *

Question: "*Are you satisfied or dissatisfied with the progress that the U.N. has made to date?*"

Date	% Satisfied	% Dissatisfied
Apr. 1946	37	37
June 1946	26	49
Nov. 1946	27	43
Dec. 1946	39	33
Apr. 1947	26	50
Aug. 1947	24	51
Sep. 1947	33	51
May 1948	21	54

* Material adapted from polls taken by the American Institute of Public Opinion.

ous references to the United Nations in the general context of foreign affairs and national security. In a series of three surveys made by the American Institute of Public Opinion national samples were asked: "If Russia continues to follow her present course what should we do, if anything?" In March, 1946, 8 per cent volunteered the proposal that the United States should "go before the UN"; in July, 1947, 4 per cent made this proposal; and in March, 1948, only 1 per cent referred to the United Nations.[23] Most of the respondents recommended a policy of firm resistance or measures of national defense, or more recently, preparations for war or resort to war. These figures are perhaps more reliable indications of the degree to which the United Nations is viewed as a significant instrument in American security policy by the general public. One might say, then, that sanguine expectations of the efficacy of the United Nations as an instrument of American security are now held only by a small though militant minority of Americans. An earlier mood of benevolent skepticism which did not place too great hopes on an international security agency now seems to have been supplanted by dissatisfaction with, or indifference to, the United Nations as an instrument of national security. Since hopes were apparently never very high, the disenchantment has remained within moderate limits. There has been no revulsion against the United Nations. In the public mind, continued participation in, and support of, this agency has a conscience-appeasing function. At the same time that we take realistic measures intended to protect our interests we maintain a peripheral contact with the kingdom. In this connection a *Fortune* poll released in February, 1948, showed 55 per cent of a national sample supporting the position that "America should continue to count on the United Nations and do all it can to make it work." Only 10 per cent thought the United States should give up its participation in the United Nations in favor of "separate alliances with friendly nations." Twenty per cent approved the statement that the United States should "start plans for a world government in which various countries will become member states." Other recent polls show a readiness to support specific measures intended to strengthen the United Nations.[24] However, the ambivalence of American attitudes toward ceding sovereignty to a world organization is reflected in a survey conducted by the Roper organization for *Time*. A national sample was asked, "If we were to have voting power in proportion to our population and economic strength, would you like to see us join now with other democratic countries to make a United States of the world?" Forty-three per cent answered favorably, while 38 per cent were opposed and 19 per cent were noncommittal. However, when those favoring American participation in a world government were asked the further question, "Would you be in favor of joining this

United States of the world if it meant giving control of the atom bomb to the new organization?" only 22 per cent remained resolute.[25]

Mass opinion in the United States on the issue of universal conscription has not in any direct sense constituted an obstacle to the institution of such a program. Since December of 1942 the proportion favoring universal military training has never dropped below 60 per cent.[26] But this approval should not be confused with active advocacy. The ardent advocates have largely been on the other side. Minority groups of pacifists, and influential sectors of the religious and educational elites have been able to resist the institution of universal conscription because of the passivity and low intensity of general public approval.

Several surveys made during the course of the past year reflect overwhelming public support of the American program of rearmament. While a larger proportion favors increases in the air force rather than in either of the other services, the doctrine of a "balanced defense establishment" seems to be reflected in a comparatively large-scale approval of increases in the other branches. Some of this enthusiasm for national defense could still be dispelled in 1948 by the suggestion that such increases would mean a heavier tax load. But even when the individual costs to the taxpayer were made explicit, 63 per cent still favored a larger air force, 55 per cent a larger navy, and 55 per cent a larger army.[27] A *Fortune* survey released in June, 1948, showed that over 80 per cent favored increases in American military strength.

American opinion accords support to the North Atlantic Pact and the program of aid associated with it. Well over two-thirds of the respondents in a group of surveys favored our assumption of the North Atlantic commitment.[28] A somewhat smaller number but still a substantial majority favored giving arms aid to the Western European nations.[29]

There can also be little doubt that the public would be ready to support American commitments in Western Europe by war in the event of Soviet aggression. But the determination of what constitutes vital American interests to be defended by military means if necessary is a decision which the public tends to leave to its policy-makers. Thus, after official statements were made of our intention to remain in Berlin despite the Soviet blockade, 80 per cent of a national sample were ready to support this policy even if it were to result in war. On the other hand, only a minority in several national surveys favored strong measures to resist Communist expansion in China.[30] Had the administration proposed a strong China policy, it is likely that public support would have been forthcoming.

The apparent readiness of public opinion to support the various security measures taken by the government in the past three years should not be taken to mean that the public understands the significance and implications of these policies or their relationships to one another. In the present period of overt and well-dramatized threat to American interests, public sentiment might be described as being in a state of uneasy plasticity. When a sample of respondents was asked in March, 1948, what course they considered advisable to deal with the Russian problem, the responses were of the most primitive sort, reflecting emotional states rather than a sense of policy. There were no references to the policy of containment. Only 3 per cent referred to the formation of military alliances. Another 3 per cent proposed the cessation of American shipments of goods to the Soviet Union, or "economic blockade." The absence of specific or relevant policy proposals in these spontaneous responses reflects the general role of American opinion in the present crisis. Even if interest in the foreign crisis were informed and sustained, the general public would hardly be in a position to make rational choices between alternative policies. The public apparently makes one primary requirement of American foreign policy: that it be resolute and firm in its opposition to Soviet expansion. The specific methods it leaves to the various elite groups which participate in the policy-making process. It is interesting to speculate on the question of whether these policy and opinion elites are themselves fully aware of the extent of discretion which the public accords them in the present crisis, and of how this discretion might narrow should Soviet pressure be suddenly withdrawn. American isolationism in the period between the two world wars was not only a phenomenon of mass sentiment—it was an implicit assumption of American leadership. It is entirely possible that this feeling of being limited and constrained by American opposition to "entangling alliances" continues to affect American foreign policy in the form of unconscious and traditional patterns of thinking among the policy elites. It is difficult to be rid of the memory of what was the most significant factor in American foreign policy before World War II. It is perhaps hard for a policy leadership whose area of discretion had for so long been closely confined, to utilize effectively and creatively the new freedom the public now accords it.

American Attitudes Toward Atomic Weapons

The American problem of security has not only been changed by its emergence as the sole power capable of organizing resistance to an aggressive Soviet Union: it has been transformed in the technological dimension by the discovery of atomic weapons and other developments in the technology of warfare. As the Soviet-Communist threat has become more explicit and immediate, the American public has become increasingly ready to support a resort to force in defense of its own system of values. To what extent does it recognize the full implications of such a resolution?

The general problem of American attitudes toward atomic weapons may be treated under the following headings: (1) the suppression of its threatening implications, (2) the possibility of panic at a time when the American superiority is effectively challenged, (3) attitudes toward the control of atomic energy by an international agency, (4) attitudes toward the American use of atomic weapons in warfare.

The American public is practically universally aware of the discovery of atomic weapons. In a survey conducted in 1946, 98 per cent of a national sample had heard of the atomic bomb. This is a remarkable finding, since on most public questions there is always a substantial sector which is unaware of major public events.[31] The American public is not only aware of the existence of the atomic bomb, but is also aware that it has tremendous destructive possibilities. At the same time, the American public considered it unlikely that the secret of the manufacture of the bomb could be kept by the United States for more than a few years. Many Americans, upon being questioned in 1946 and 1947, expressed the opinion that the Russians already had the secret of atomic bomb manufacture. However, the atom bomb does not seem to constitute a matter of great and conscious concern to most Americans, despite the fact that awareness is practically universal, the destructiveness of atomic weapons is generally recognized, and the impossibility of maintaining the American monopoly had been conceded.

It is noteworthy that in the "focus of attention" surveys

discussed above, only an extremely small percentage of the respondents ever referred to atomic weapons as the most important problem before the American people. The proportion typically ranged between one and five per cent. In an opinion survey in which respondents were directly asked whether they were worried about the atomic bomb, 13 per cent said they were "greatly worried," another 13 per cent were "moderately worried," and 11 per cent were "somewhat worried, but were not getting grayhaired over it." Fifty per cent claimed they weren't worried at all. But if one reads the actual comments made by respondents in their replies to this question one has the impression that many of those who "weren't worried much," or claimed "not to be worried at all" had registered the threat but had suppressed its implications into the periphery of consciousness. "I'm not worried about it. What's the use of worrying? If I did, there are other weapons which are worse being developed all the time, and I'd no sooner get over worrying about it than a worse one would come along. So what's the use." [32]

Perhaps an even larger group of Americans not only suppress the threat of the "atom bomb" from consciousness, but facilitate this process by self-deception. Not more than a fifth of the respondents in two separate surveys were ready to accept the fact generally recognized by the experts that the prospect of an effective defense against atomic weapons is extremely remote. Some 40 per cent apparently were convinced that it would be possible for the United States to develop a defense against atomic attack. Approximately one-third were undecided or didn't know. [33]

The attitude syndrome with regard to the threat of atomic weapons consists perhaps of four components. First, the psychological mechanism of suppression makes it possible to push a troublesome prospect to the periphery of awareness. Second, American optimism and trust in "know-how" leads to a widespread conviction that it "can't happen to us"— "we can lick the problem of atomic defense." A third element is the feeling of powerlessness and futility. Since the "man in the street" can do nothing about the problem, why should he worry about it? A fourth element is the indefiniteness of the prospect of atomic attack. The threat is remote; consequently, there is no need for worrying about it in the present. The second, third, and fourth attitudes all facilitate the process of suppression by providing intellectual justifications.

Together these attitude tendencies perhaps account for the unconscious "conspiracy of silence" about the atomic problem which obtains in the United States today. In the first period after Hiroshima the very drama of the discovery of atomic fission captured the imaginations of the overwhelming majority of the population. But as efforts at international control have been frustrated, and as Soviet-American relations have steadily deteriorated, thought of the bomb and its threatening implications has been pressed from the focus of attention.

The testing of an atomic weapon in the Soviet Union in August, 1949, has terminated the era of American monopoly, and has opened the phase of increasing American strategic and psychological vulnerability. It is probable that the superiority of the American stockpile of atomic weapons, of its productive capacity, and of its air power will continue for a substantial period. It is possible indeed that American superiority will continue indefinitely. But there is a point of diminishing returns in atomic superiority. This is the point at which the Soviet Union has a sufficient stockpile and carrying power to constitute a large-scale threat to the

United States. From a political and psychological point of view, the approximation of this stage in atomic weapon competition means that future crises of United States-Russian relations will increasingly come to carry the connotation for Americans of immediate threat of vast and unknown dimensions.

The announcement of the atomic explosion in the Soviet Union was handled with great wisdom and foresight. The fact that it was first announced by the United States created confidence in the American intelligence apparatus. The handling of the announcement by the press suggests effective preparation as to the implications of this development. But the overt calm with which the announcement was received should not mislead us into believing that Americans were indifferent either to the announcement or to the threat. Perhaps it would be more accurate to describe the underlying reaction as one of helpless anxiety and dependence. The sense of vulnerability has increased, and it is perhaps necessary to plan for a generally heightened lability in mass reactions to foreign policy crises. Because of the dimensions of the threat and the meaninglessness of individual efforts to cope with it, the American public feels itself to be completely in the hands of its political and military leaders. To attempt to deal with future contingencies through policy improvisations is to incur the risk of sudden mass reactions. Here as never before, only a unified leadership capable of dispassionate planning and resolution can hold these reactions in check and point them in such constructive directions as will enhance the interests of nation and humanity.

From the very beginning the American public has demonstrated considerable ambivalence on the score of voluntarily sharing its atomic secrets with other countries. It apparently still insists on the maintenance of some measure of its immediate short-run advantage. On the simple question of control of atomic factories in the United States by an international agency narrow majorities appear to have been in favor during 1947.[34] When this general question was made more specific by adding the qualification that all countries including the U.S. would have to permit "UN inspectors to see if each country is living up to its agreements," a much greater majority during 1947 favored international control—67 per cent in February, 1947, and 79 per cent in October, 1947. Apparently at this time, specification of the multilateral character of international inspection produced greater confidence. But this confidence seems to have declined rapidly. In May, 1948, only 43 per cent favored control when confronted with a similarly worded question.[35]

And even during 1947, when such substantial majorities favored effective inspection of atomic facilities, most Americans were either opposed or undecided on the question of instituting a plan of atomic control which would require the United States to destroy its stock of bombs. In February, 49 per cent, and in October, 52 per cent drew the line on this yielding up of an immediate American advantage. Majorities were prepared to approve a policy of stopping the manufacture of atomic bombs, but only minorities were ready to destroy existing stocks.[36] Similarly only a minority (41 per cent) was ready to give an international agency "all the information it needs about atomic energy." [37]

This ambivalence was linked with a general skepticism about the prospects of instituting a system of international control. In October, 1947, only 14 per cent thought the prospect was "good," 35 per cent rated the prospect as "only fair," and 36 per cent called it "poor." [38] The general confusion and instability of American views on the control of atomic energy is reflected in sharp differences apparently resulting from the wording of questions. This type of instability reflects what the public opinion specialists refer to as "unstructured opinion." Most Americans were quite undecided about how to cope with the problem of atomic weapons. They recognized the temporary character of American monopoly and the great risks involved in an atomic weapons race. They were ready to favor efforts at effective international control, but had great doubts about their success. Under these circumstances they tended to support the principle of international control, but hedged at yielding up immediate American advantages. It is still too early to judge the effects of Russian atomic developments on the American attitude toward the control of atomic energy.

A fourth important opinion problem growing out of the discovery of atomic weapons is the question of whether moral conflict and inhibition among the American people might in any way limit the use of atomic weapons in warfare. We have in the atomic weapon an instrumentality of *catastrophic* and *random* destructive power. By its very nature it cannot be specifically directed toward physical installations or the armed forces of enemy nations. Quite without regard to military intent it is a weapon which will hit "civilian" targets, and with terroristic consequences. There can be little question that in atomic weapons we have instrumentalities so destructive in character as to inhibit their use except under extraordinary circumstances.

From the available evidence, what are the circumstances which might justify the use of atomic weapons? First, it appears that only a minority of Americans felt particularly guilty about the use of atomic bombs against Hiroshima and Nagasaki. In September, 1945, only 31 per cent of a national sample picked answers in a multiple-choice question suggesting criticism of the use of atomic bombs in the Japanese war: 4 per cent felt that we should not have used them at all; 27 per cent thought we ought to have used them by way of a demonstration of American power in areas where there were no people. Forty-three per cent approved the "bombing of one city at a time" in order to provide opportunities for surrender in between bombings. A somewhat bloodthirsty 24 per cent picked the answer suggesting indiscriminate use of the atomic weapon.[39] These figures were roughly confirmed by a *Fortune* survey.[40] The latter survey suggested an even greater proportion which approved of our wartime use of the atomic bomb, and just about the same percentage approved the more destructive course of using "many more of them before Japan had a chance to surrender."

These figures suggest that in a destructive war of "no quarter" when ordinary explosives were already achieving devastating effects, and when American hate of Japan was at a high pitch, the use of weapons of this type did not appear to leave any particular residue of guilt. From the American point of view the Japanese had read themselves out of any moral community by atrocities against civilian populations and American troops, and by the suicidal nature of the Japanese resistance. The atom bombing of Japan could be justified to the satisfaction of most Americans as a method of saving American lives. But this Japanese experience does not help us very much in speculating about American attitudes toward the use of atomic weapons in a future war situation. There can be little doubt that moral conflict would play a role of some importance in future war crises if and when they arise.

This is suggested by a tendency on the part of many

Americans to reject the atom bomb, to wish that it had never been invented. Two surveys—one conducted in October, 1945, the other in August, 1947—reflect this state of mind. In October, 1945, some 30 per cent "wished that we had never discovered the atomic bomb." In October, 1947, 38 per cent felt this way. Another survey made in 1946, and consequently out of date, specifically attempted to find out under what conditions Americans would be ready to launch a "preventive" atomic attack.[41] Since the sample was small it would be wrong to attach too much importance to the precise precentages. The question was as follows:

> "If we ever suspect that a certain country is planning to make a surprise atomic bomb attack on our country within a few days, which one of these two things do you think we should do?
>
> "We should try to keep from being the first country to be bombed even if this means starting an atomic war on them as soon as we become suspicious."   47%
> "We should try to prove if they're really planning this attack even if waiting means taking a chance that we'll be bombed first."   43%
> "Don't know."   10%

It is on the whole likely that the deterioration of international relations in the past two years has reduced the number of those who would want to become quite certain of the enemy's intention before launching a preventive atomic attack. Certainly very few Americans today favor the policy of "waiting until some other nation has used it on us first." [42] In a recent poll only 20 per cent favored such extreme restrictions on the use of the weapon; 70 per cent were opposed. What the present evidence seems to suggest is that the American conscience is unlikely to support a preventive atomic attack unless it is, or is made to appear as, an attack intended to forestall such an attack on the United States.

This, to be sure quite speculative, judgment suggests that for the present period of international relations the atom bomb has a limited value as an instrument of American foreign policy. In the period of great American superiority it can only serve as a deterrent against overt aggression on the part of the Soviet Union. But it is not the kind of instrument that we can use against Communist-initiated strikes in Western European countries, against Communist coups in Eastern Europe, against Communist guerrilla warfare in Greece, or against campaigns of native Communist armies in China or other parts of the Far East. The Soviet Union can probably count on our incapacity to employ this weapon against her except under two sets of circumstances: (1) overt Soviet aggression in areas where the United States has assumed firm commitments, (2) at a time when the Soviet atomic threat to the United States seems to be a good deal more immediate than it is today. In the absence of either the one or the other of these circumstances Russia would appear to be free from the threat of atomic attack. What ties the hands of American policy aside from expediential calculations appears to be the morally crushing choice of using catastrophic and random means of destruction without a provocation or a threat of comparable dimensions.

VI. Social Groupings and the Foreign Policy Mood

THE trends of foreign policy opinion so far described have reflected changes in attitude among the general population in the postwar period. Are these attitudes proportionally distributed within the various strata of the population, or are there significant attitude differences which are associated with social and economic characteristics? Unfortunately, most attitude surveys lack realistic political criteria for the determination of the universe to be sampled and its internal structure. The role of individuals as policy-makers in the real world is not equal; and only a very extreme conception of the democratic doctrine requires that they be so. The pollers have not effectively faced the problem of social and political structure. They have only begun to adapt their techniques to the actual distribution of influence and interest. Just as polling is likely to profit greatly by the introduction of psychological insights [1] and techniques, so would it gain in realism and usefulness if it were to develop sociological and political sophistication.

The tools for a more refined analysis of opinions and attitudes in relation to social and political structure are at least in part available and have been put to limited use.[2] There is every prospect that these shortcomings will be recognized as the sample survey technique becomes assimilated into the social sciences. With all their limitations the polls provide us with practically the only quantitative data available, not only on "general opinion," but also on political attitudes among different sectors of the population. What has been forgotten in the reaction which followed the November, 1948, election is that other types of material on the attitudes of social groups present even greater problems of reliability than do the polls.

From the existing sample breakdowns it is possible in a rough sort of way to suggest some hypotheses as to significant differences in the foreign policy mood among the various groupings in the population. A limited amount of the available polling data has been reported with breakdowns based on age, sex, income groups, occupation, education, and region. Analysis of the foreign policy attitudes of these population groups tends to confirm some popular conceptions and to invalidate others. It also suggests a number of novel hypotheses.

Age and Sex

In general there would appear to be substantial homogeneity in the foreign policy attitudes of the various age groups in the United States. While differences have been reported they do not reflect a serious "problem of generations." Those that appear to exist can be accounted for by the special experience of the younger age groups. It might be said that for persons under thirty years of age the most vivid political recollections have to do with foreign policy— the crisis of international politics from the late 1930's until the outbreak of war, the war experience itself, and the postwar foreign policy controversies. The "depression trauma" of the early 'thirties is a remote childhood memory for most of the younger generation while it still continues to affect the political judgment of the older age groups. In addition, one might expect among the older age groups a greater measure of skepticism about the effectiveness of international organization and a greater emphasis on unilateral and multilateral security arrangements as a consequence of their longer experience span. More of them will vividly recall the failure of the League of Nations and of collective security and continue to harbor the disillusionments of the interwar period. Then too, age itself often tends to sober idealism and inhibit transports of hope. Among the younger age groups the immediacy of their school experience also affects foreign policy judgment. It is perhaps true that the secondary schools and most of the colleges tend to stress international organization and foreign policy idealism at the expense of security considerations. From the point of view of pedagogy it is simpler to discuss the structure of the United Nations than world politics. Such institutional arrangements have the kind of specificity which is easily taught and remembered. In addition, there tends to be an ethical revulsion against "power politics" and "national security" among many, perhaps most, school teachers and college instructors. Factors of age, experience, and training, thus, suggest three hypotheses as to foreign policy differences among the American generations: (1) the younger groups are likely to set a greater priority on international affairs than on domestic; (2) they are likely to be more informed on the organizational aspects of international relations; (3) they are more likely to be optimistic about the prospects of international organization and less likely to favor unilateral security actions.

The available data on the attitudes of younger people toward foreign policy problems suggest the validity of these three hypotheses. A substantial 9 per cent more people under the age of twenty-one than over twenty-one were aware of the fact that the United States had joined an organization working for international peace. Substantially fewer of those under twenty-one (again a difference of 9 per cent) were aware of the fact that the United States was providing financial and military aid to Greece.[3] The awareness of foreign affairs by persons of school age was biased in favor of international, and against security, measures. Similarly, the younger age groups stressed international problems as being of most importance to the United States. Fifteen per cent more of those between the ages of fourteen and twenty listed foreign policy as the major problem facing the United States.[4] In connection with the presidential election of 1948, 57 per cent of those between the ages of twenty-one and thirty-four emphasized the importance of having a president skilled in international affairs, as compared with 49 per cent for the older age groups.[5] Substantially fewer of the younger age groups showed isolationist tendencies. In a Survey Research Center poll conducted in the fall of 1948 it was found that only slightly more than a quarter of the respondents between the ages of twenty and thirty-four thought the "United States had gone too far in concerning itself with problems in other parts of the world." Well over a third of the respondents in the age range of fifty-five and over took this moderately isolationist position.[6]

The greater preference among younger people for solutions of problems through international agencies and their greater tendency to reject unilateral security arrangements is also suggested by the evidence. Fifty-three per cent of those between the ages of twenty-one and thirty-nine wanted international trade regulated by the United Nations, as compared with 41 per cent of those forty years of age and over.[7] In general, the younger age groups displayed a greater generosity with respect to foreign economic policy. Respondents under thirty years of age more frequently approved sending large sums of money for the rehabilitation of war-torn Europe.[8] The percentage of those in the younger age groups who wanted to rely on world organization rather than superior military force as a means of protecting American security was significantly greater than among the older generation. Similarly, a larger percentage of the age group twenty-one to thirty-nine was susceptible to "world government" proposals.

There appears to be a greater readiness among the younger survey respondents to give Russia the "benefit of the doubt" and, related to this reaction, a greater opposition to preventive war. Sixty per cent of the respondents under thirty years of age in a Survey Research Center poll oppose going to war with Russia "before they are able to make atomic bombs." Less than half of the respondents over forty-five years of age were opposed to preventive war under these conditions.[9] It is also of interest that the younger age groups appear to be more susceptible to panic. Thus, immediately after the onset of the Berlin blockade crisis, a substantially higher proportion (34 per cent) of the younger respondents expected war "within one or two years." The proportion expecting war within this period among the older age groups was approximately 10 per cent lower.[10]

The comparatively small deviation in the foreign policy attitudes of the younger age groups as one might expect lies in the direction of a greater foreign policy idealism and optimism. The climate of opinion during their upbringing, their youthful enthusiasm, and perhaps a certain bias in their schooling may account for this tendency.

The foreign policy attitudes of American men and women also tend to be homogeneous. On such questions as expectations of war and military conscription the differences between the sexes are not statistically significant. However, there are three respects in which women appear to differ from men in their foreign policy attitudes. First, more women than men seem to be ignorant of or apathetic to foreign policy issues. There are consistently more "don't know's," "no opinion's" and "undecided's" among women. The differences in this regard are quite high, ranging from 10 to 20 per cent. Second, more women tend to be "idealistic" and "internationalist" in their attitudes toward foreign affairs. Eight per cent more women preferred reliance on the United Nations to American military power as a means of attaining security.[11] And 9 per cent more women than men opposed a policy of isolationism in the postwar period.[12] Third, more women than men among the respondents favored the continuance of a friendly approach toward Russia and opposed the "get tough with Russia" policy.[13] This evidence as to the greater prevalence of idealistic foreign policy attitudes among women gives some support to Gorer's thesis regarding the moral role of the female in America. At the same time, the comparatively small percentage differences hardly justify the extreme sex-related moral dualism which he proposes.[14]

Thus the polls give some support to the popular impression that youth and women are more susceptible to pacifist, internationalist, and "world government" arguments. Contrariwise, the hypothesis might be advanced that nationalist, isolationist, and preventive war appeals have greater resonance among the males of the older generations. Nevertheless, these differences are not to be viewed as major cleavages within the population as a whole, but rather as relatively small differences of degree. At the level of activism and leadership, however, these differences perhaps assume a greater importance. It is probably correct that the leadership and active membership of "idealistic" foreign policy organizations (e.g., pacifists and world federalists) are predominantly female and youthful, while the leadership and active membership of the nationalist and reactionary organizations tend to be recruited from the older males.

Social Class and Foreign Policy

A recent study of the psychological characteristics of social classes in the United States made by Richard Centers of Princeton University suggests a number of quite significant hypotheses as to the relationships between economic position, basic attitudes, and foreign policy attitudes.[15] The middle and working classes in the United States appear to differ significantly in their expectations of the future and their feelings of relatedness to, and capacity to master, "life." While it is in general correct to say that the "effort-optimism" syndrome referred to at an earlier point continues to be a matter of faith among a very large element of the American population (including a majority of the working classes), it is clearly more characteristic of the middle and upper classes than of the working classes. On a question as to "why people succeed" almost 69 per cent of the middle-class sample attributed success to ability or ability plus other factors such as luck, "pull," better opportunities, etc. Only 52 per cent of the working-class sample in this recent study viewed ability, or ability in combination with other factors, as the basis of success. More of the working-class sample were dissatisfied with their jobs, their pay, their own opportunities, their chances to enjoy life.

Centers also compared the social classes with regard to their attitudes toward values. His most interesting finding was that the middle classes more frequently stressed "self-expression" as a value, while the working classes appeared "to prefer security." The differences were quite substantial. Sixty per cent of the middle-class sample picked self-expression as one of their three highest values, as compared with 44 per cent for the working-class group. Only 27 per cent of the middle-class sample listed security as one of their three most important objectives, while 53 per cent of the working-class sample preferred security. These findings suggest the broader hypothesis that the middle classes in the United States have a greater and more complex sense of relatedness and involvement with the world. They perhaps tend to be more creative, also more flexible and dynamic in their views of their potentialities. The stress on security among the working classes suggests a tendency to withdraw, an atrophy of value potentialities, an acceptance of minimum life aims. These, of course, are differences of degree. It is important not to overlook the very large overlapping and homogeneity in values among the social classes.

The data also suggest a greater tendency toward pessimism, bitterness, and cynicism among the lower-income groups. The middle classes, at least overtly, are the primary bearers of the American myth of opportunity and advancement. Unfortunately, Centers' study just skims the surface of the problem. It tells us little of the psychological structure of American optimism, how much of it is a suppressed fear of failure, how much of the surface motion and amiability grows out of inner feelings which are quite different in quality and intensity.

The polling data available on the foreign policy attitudes of American income and occupational groups is on the whole consistent with these general findings.[16] The lower-income groups appear to be poorly informed about foreign affairs. More of these elements fall consistently into the "don't know" and "no opinion" categories in the polling reports.[17] They are less frequently members of organizations which discuss political and international problems. Members of the lower-income groups more frequently tend to view the future of international relations with a kind of fatalistic resignation, in contrast to the moderate optimism which is more characteristic of the middle and wealthy groups. Thus, on a question as to whether the United States could do anything to prevent war, only 46 per cent of the lower-income groups thought anything could be done, in contrast to 59 per cent for the middle-income groups and 62 per cent for the upper-income groups.[18] (See Table VI.)

There also would appear to be a greater tendency toward nationalism and isolationism among the lower-income classes. Thus, on the issue of whether the United States should follow an isolationist or an internationalist policy only 57 per cent of the lower-income sample favored an international outlook, as compared with 74 per cent for the middle-income groups and over 80 per cent for the wealthy.[19] Similarly only 26 per cent of the lower-class sample approved the joining of an organization by the United States in which it would have to abide by majority rule, as compared with 43 per cent for the middle-income group and 49 per cent for the wealthy.[20]

Analysis of the attitudes of the various occupational groupings tends to confirm these findings. Thus, professional persons and executives have the same attitudes as the upper-income groups. They are the most informed sector of the American population, the most interested in foreign affairs, the least pessimistic about the prospects for peace, and the most optimistic with regard to the capacity of the United States to develop policies which might prevent war. At the other end of the scale, unskilled and semiskilled labor, do-

TABLE VI

INCOME GROUPS AND FOREIGN POLICY *

Questions	Upper	Middle	Lower
% who say the United States must buy abroad in order to sell abroad (Aug. '46)..	83	79	67
% who belong to groups or organizations which discuss national and international problems (May '47)..................	28	16	8
% who think there is something the United States could do to prevent a war † (May '47)................................	62	59	46
% who approve of this country's joining a "majority rule" type of world organization (Feb. '47).......................	49	43	26
% who disapproved of the idea of the U.S. withdrawing from the world (Feb. '47)...	86	74	57
% who advocate a high tariff policy for United States (Aug. '46)..............	53	53	42
† % who gave "No Opinion" or "Don't Know" answers....................	10	13	22

The Survey Research Center states its income categories numerically. The three groups are: under $2000, $2000-$3999, $4000 and over. The National Opinion Research Center uses the following breakdown:

A. This group is drawn from among those people who, in their respective communities, comprise the top 2 per cent of the families, arranged according to their wealth or economic prosperity.

B. This group is drawn from the next 14 per cent of families.

C. This group is drawn from the next lower 52 per cent of families.

D. This group is drawn from the lowest 32 per cent of families.

The NORC combines the two upper categories.

The Institute of Public Opinion (Gallup) relies on the interviewer's judgment of the level of consumption of the respondents

* Tables VI, VII, and VIII are adapted from public opinion polls of the American Institute of Public Opinion, the *Fortune* survey, and the National Opinion Research Center.

mestic servants, and farmers are the least informed group in foreign policy matters, the least interested in international issues, the most pessimistic about efforts to maintain peace, and the most inclined toward nationalist and isolationist attitudes. While it is important to stress that the percentage of overlapping among occupational groups is considerably greater than the percentage of deviation, nevertheless the differences are significant and have important implications for public information policy.

These class-related differences in foreign policy attitudes appear to be consistent with the general psychological characteristics of the various social classes. A greater frequency of pessimism about personal prospects among the lower classes may be related to a greater frequency of pessimism about international prospects. Personal moods and expectations color general political moods and expectations. A greater degree of frustration of aspirations produces resentment and hostility reactions which may bias some members of the lower classes in the direction of a hard nationalism. Thus respondents in lower-income groups more frequently opposed giving financial aid to foreign countries. A greater tendency toward apathy and withdrawal in the personal sense among the lower classes may produce a bias in the direction of political withdrawal or isolationism.

Education

Since education tends to be closely correlated with social class it might have been expected that the distribution of foreign policy attitudes in the educational and income pyramids would be quite similar. However, the contrasts between the college-educated and the grade school levels are much sharper than those observed among the upper- and lower-income groups. The college-educated group constitutes an intellectual stratum which is concentrated among the upper- and middle-income groups, and among persons carrying on professional or executive occupations. This college-trained, upper-income, "mental-worker" stratum of the population is the most alert, informed, interested, and discriminating audience for public policy decisions. This is the "attentive" audience for foreign policy discussion. In America this is a large group consisting of several millions. It is quite heterogeneous in its social, economic, and political composition. While the degree to which high school and grade school education are correlated with middle- and lower-income status respectively is not clear, there can be little question that proportionately more in the middle groups have had the advantages of high school education, and proportionately more in the lower-income group have been limited to grade school education. Thus the "lower-income—grade school—unskilled and semi-skilled workers and farmers" constitute a stratum of the population which tends to be inert and apathetic, a group which is most readily manipulated by organizational bureaucracies such as church and trade-union leaderships.

Characteristically there were between twice and three times as many "don't know's" and "no opinion's" among those limited to grade school education as there were among the college educated. Those who had completed high school were an intermediate group. On questions involving knowledge of facts affecting foreign policy it was found that the college-educated contained four or five times as many informed persons as the grade school sample. More than 30 per cent of the college-educated sample belonged to organizations in which international problems were discussed, in comparison with only 15 per cent for the high school group, and 7 per cent for the grade school sample.[21] (See Table VII.) Substantially more of the grade school group showed isolationist and nationalist tendencies. More of them were reluctant to give financial support to the United Nations. Although the proportion was small (13 per cent), substantially more persons of grade school education favored a policy of "not having anything to do with the rest of the world."[22] Only 1 per cent of the college educated favored this position. While 54 per cent of the college educated approved American participation in a world organization based on majority rule, only 30 per cent of the grade school group were ready to accept this limitation on national power.[23]

The grade school sample was also inclined to be more pessimistic about the future. Only 47 per cent [24] felt that the United States could do anything to prevent a war, as compared with 71 per cent among the college educated. The grade school group also was most pessimistic about relations with Russia.

Questions which were quite revealing of attitude differences between the college and grade school educated were those having to do with the United Nations. The college educated were ready to go farthest in according power and financial support to the United Nations. At the same time they were the least satisfied with its progress. The grade school group was less disposed to make sacrifices for the establishment of a world organization, and also was least dissatisfied with its progress. It had made only a small investment of hope, and consequently tended to be indifferent to the small dividends of accomplishment which the United Nations yielded. In general, these data tend to support the hypothesis that among the poorly educated, lower-income manual workers the sense of involvement in public, and

TABLE VII

EDUCATIONAL BACKGROUND AND FOREIGN POLICY

Questions	College	High School	Grade School
% who show a reasonably correct understanding of what a tariff is (Aug. '46)	64	50	22
% who belong to groups or organizations which discuss national and international problems (May '47)	32	15	7
% who are dissatisfied with the progress the United Nations has made so far * (June '46)	69	53	42
% who believe the United States should remain in the United Nations in spite of Russian behavior (Aug. '47)	91	81	63
% who think there is something the United States can do to prevent a war (May '47) . .	71	54]	47]
% who think the United States should maintain a force larger than an international police force (May '47)	20	33	36
% who think Russia will co-operate with us in world affairs (Dec. '46)	60	49	35
% who feel it would be a good idea to have reciprocal trade agreements with foreign countries † (June '45)	81	67	43
% who approve of this government keeping to itself and not having anything to do with the rest of the world (Feb. '47)	1	7	13
% who approve this country's joining a "majority rule" type of world organization (Feb. '47)	54	38	30
* % who gave "No Opinion" or "Don't Know" answers	8	21	32
† % who gave "No Opinion" or "Don't Know" answers	10	24	49

particularly international, affairs tends to be extremely limited and passive.

It is a great temptation to attribute these differences in political attitudes which are associated with income, occupation, and education, to "lack of information," or "areas of ignorance." The policy implications of such an interpretation are clear and simple. Lack of information can be remedied by more information; and "areas of ignorance" can be dispelled by civic-minded campaigns of public education. In actuality the problem runs a great deal deeper. A discriminating analysis of the evidence suggests that a large sector of the lower-income, poorly educated majority of the population is incapable of assimilating the materials of informational campaigns. Its basic apathy is a consequence of emotional and social conditions. Its intellectual horizon tends to be quite limited, and its analytical skill is rudimentary. It will take a great deal more than public relations to remedy such a situation and produce the degree of involvement and activism which is characteristic of the upper educational and income groups. Actually no one has proposed a solution to this basic problem which is not transparently inadequate or obviously Utopian. In Karl Mannheim's terms, the rationality of the modern urban-industrial masses is "functional" and passive in nature.[25] That is to say, their activities tend to be rationally co-ordinated in complex industrial and bureaucratic divisions of labor in which policy is made by a remote center, whether it be the management elite or the trade-union leadership.[26] Thus, according to Mannheim, there is a cultural impairment of the capacity for moral autonomy and intellectual independence implicit in the socio-economic system. Persons who tend to be objects of remote decision and manipulation in their private lives are unlikely to approach problems of public policy with a sense of mastery and independence.

Region

Regional differences in foreign policy attitudes were quite pronounced in the period before World War II, but the evidence for the period since Pearl Harbor shows regional differences to be of declining importance. In a *Fortune* poll released in July, 1940, almost 42 per cent of the Middle Western sample were not only opposed to involvement in the "shooting" war, but were against coming to the aid of England in any form. In contrast, only 15 per cent of the New England and Middle Atlantic respondents took this position of complete neutrality. The respondents from the Southern and Southwestern states were more frequently ready to go to war if necessary to prevent the defeat of the Allies.

In general, this was the regional pattern of foreign policy attitudes in the prewar period. The Middle Western states were consistently less ready to take active steps of an economic or military character in the support of the Allies. The Northeast and the West were moderately interventionist, while the South was exceptionally interventionist. The Middle West deviated in the isolationist direction on the average by around 8 to 10 per cent. The South deviated in an interventionist direction on the average by more than 15 per cent.

Since the shock of Pearl Harbor and the experience of the war, foreign policy attitudes in the various regions have been remarkably similar. Most of the differences have been statistically insignificant. In some cases the Middle Western respondents have shown themselves to be more "internationalist" than the respondents from other regions. The only evidence of the persistence of prewar attitudes in the Middle West is the greater degree of opposition to universal conscription. In this regard the Middle Western respondents lagged behind the other regions by about 6 per cent. On questions involving information about foreign affairs, the Middle West and particularly the South seem to have lagged behind the other regions.

The South now appears to be the region characterized by the greatest deviation in foreign policy attitudes. These differences have been substantial on issues involving foreign trade. The Southern respondents were more in favor of low tariffs by 10 per cent over the other regions.[27] (See Table VIII.) Also 10 per cent more among the Southern sample were opposed to international regulation of foreign trade.[28] In the first case the Southern respondents appear to be following the traditional position of their region. The second case may reflect feeling in the South that international regulation of foreign trade might reduce the market for the staple Southern crops such as cotton.

Although regional differences in foreign policy attitudes no longer appear to be of great importance, there are significant urban-rural differences. The rural population is more traditionalist and less exposed to the pressure of the media of communication. The rural population is less attentive to problems of foreign affairs. They have less information on world politics; fewer of them belong to organizations in which foreign affairs are discussed. More of them were "undecided," or refused to express an opinion when confronted with foreign policy questions.[29]

The evidence also suggests that the rural population is more pessimistic than the urban and has less of a sense of power to influence events. Thus, when asked whether anything could be done by the United States to prevent war, fewer of the rural respondents had confidence either in their

TABLE VIII

REGIONAL BREAKDOWNS AND FOREIGN POLICY

Questions	N.E. & M.A.	Mid-west	South	Far West
% who think it would be best for the U.S. to participate in world affairs (Feb. '46)	71	72	69	77
% who think there is something the United States could do to prevent a war (May '47)	60	53	55	50
% who would strengthen U.N. by giving it control of all armed forces (July '46)	51	56	56	57
% who think the U.S. should maintain a force larger than an international police force (May '47)	28	28	37	33
% who favor peacetime military conscription (Aug. '47)	68	59	66	70
% who believe the U.S. should rely on world organization rather than the atomic bomb for defense (Feb. '46)	57	51	48	54
% who said trade should be regulated by the United Nations (Aug. '46)	48	50	40	49
% who wanted a low tariff policy (Aug. '46)	46	48	59	45

own capacity or in that of their government to influence events.[30]

It would appear that the more extreme American foreign policy attitudes tend to be concentrated in particular strata of the population. While the population as a whole fluctuates between a series of poles in response to external events, certain strata tend to be persistently more frequent bearers of deviational attitudes. In brief summary, one may classify young people, women, the upper-income groups, the college-educated, and the urban population as more inclined to foreign policy idealism, optimism, and internationalism. The older generations, the males, the lower-income groups, those with grade school education, and the rural population tend to be more inclined to cynicism, pessimism, isolationism, and nationalism.

A number of qualifications must be attached to so simple and sweeping a proposition. In the first place, the great overlapping among age, sex, class, education, and regional groupings must be stressed again. By a large margin they are more like one another than they are different. Within this area of overlap one notes a balancing at any given time between polar attitudes. The great mass of all social groupings reconciles idealism-cynicism, optimism-pessimism, and isolationism-internationalism in what one may describe as a time- and situation-bound "realism." Thus to be a realist within the framework of American attitudes in the pre-World War II period was to be opposed to foreign "entanglements"; in the present era it implies a recognition of the importance of the American stake in foreign affairs. To be a realist in the pre-World War II period meant to refuse to loan money to countries which had defaulted in their war debts; to be a realist today implies a readiness for financial sacrifice in the interest of American security. To be a realist in the earlier period meant to be a cynic about European power politics; to be a realist today means to be ready to participate in power politics, to encourage unification and integration. These movements of attitude among the population as a whole set up norms which in turn define the deviations. Just as the norms change from time to time, so do the deviations. The deviations occur among all sectors of the population, but more frequently among certain sociological and ideological groupings.

VII. The Elites and Foreign Policy

THE term "elite" acquired its modern sociological con- notation in the writings of Vilfredo Pareto.[1] Pareto was one of the most original and systematic thinkers in the late nineteenth- and early twentieth-century school of disillu- sionment and "scientism" which produced so many brilliant insights into, and so many distorted interpretations of, human and social behavior. Their hearts hardened by the fate of nineteenth-century liberal and socialist idealism and thrilled by the achievements of the physical and biological sciences, these intellectuals put on the white coats of the laboratory and fell to work dissecting the social organism and analyzing the physics of the soul. Their iconoclasm and detachment were somehow a suitable answer to Victorian morality and cosmology. Not many social scientists today can write of themselves as Pareto did in the opening words of his theoretical introduction: "This book is written for an exclusively scientific end. . . . I have no other purpose but objectively to seek the truth."[2] The illusion of scientific precision and theoretical comprehensiveness was often created by the application of natural science concepts to social and psychological phenomena, as in Pareto's physio- logical interpretation of social mobility, or in Freud's physi- cal and biological psychology.

The shortcomings of Pareto's elite theory resulted in part from his cynicism, and in part from his physiological bias. His doctrine rules out the possibility of a relationship of responsibility between elite and rank and file; the only possible relationship is one of coercion and manipulation. Humanitarianism in Pareto is treated as a symptom of elite degeneracy. A new elite capable of ruthlessness will soon supplant it. He also greatly oversimplified the processes of social and political mobility. He likened the "circulation of the elite" to the circulation of the blood. One gets the impression of a homogeneous substance, following certain natural laws of movement in which there is no place for the category of rational control and policy-making.

The concept of the elite as used here is not inconsistent with democratic or any other forms of control. It rests upon the insight so well established in political and sociological theory that any social form of action involves division of labor and division of influence. The influential are the elite. In a democratic society most adult persons have formally an equal share of influence. The distribution of power thus involves a gradation of influence in which there is no "non-elite" in the formal sense.[3]

Both the "elitists" and their democratic critics have created serious confusion: the first, by the rejection of the possibility of a form of political division of labor in which the people have an effective share of influence; the second, by slurring over the reality of the political and social stratification of influence and perpetuating the myth of the active "demos." A genuine understanding of the political process requires the elimination of both of these normative inhibitions and the acceptance of structural conceptions. Much of the contemporary writing on public opinion and foreign policy falls into the democratic error of minimizing the inherent social and political stratification of influence. The tendency is to pose the problem in terms of an interplay between an official democratically selected leadership and an undifferentiated public. The types of problems treated fall into two categories: first, how to make the official leadership responsible to the public; and second, how to make the public alert, informed, and active in policy-making.[4]

Actually the problems of public opinion and foreign policy are a good deal more complex than is suggested in the recent literature. As a crude approximation of political reality one might suggest four principal factors in the opinion and policy process. One may speak of a "general public" if one keeps in mind that while it is characterized by a sense of identification and reacts to general stimuli, it also contains a variety of interests and groupings which are affected differentially by both general and specific stimuli. Second, there is an "attentive public" which is informed and interested in foreign policy problems, and which constitutes the audience for the foreign policy discussions among the elites. Third, one may speak of the policy and opinion elites, the articulate policy-bearing stratum of the population which gives structure to the public, and which provides the effective means of access to the various groupings. One might almost say "who mobilizes elites, mobilizes the public." Such a formulation would be closer to the truth than some of the more ardent claims of democratic ideologues. Finally, within the elite formations one would have to single out the legal or official policy leadership—executives, legislators, civil servants—the mode of selection and role of which are more widely understood.

With this fourfold classification of factors we can begin to understand the democratic policy-making process. In this process the general mass of the population is neither interested nor informed, and is unable continuously to be active in policy-making. If interest, knowledge, and constant participation on the part of the mass were our criteria, we would have to write off all historic democracies as something other than democratic.

There are perhaps three essential criteria of a democratic policy-making process. First, there is the requirement of formal opportunity for mass participation. Second, there is the requirement of genuine autonomy and competition among the elites. Third, there is the requirement of an attentive public—an informed and interested stratum—before whom elite discussion and controversy take place. The various elites exercise different types of power in the policy-making process and have different types of relationships with their "constituencies." They impinge on policy-making at different points; and they are subject to popular control in differing degrees. The "masses" participate in policy-making in indirect and primarily passive ways. Their moods, interests, and expectations set limits on the discretion of their representatives—those exercising influence within private organizations and institutions and in the media of communication, as well as those holding public office. The public also affects the selection of elites through the public electoral process, the private electoral process of interest groups, or through "buying" or refusing to "buy" the policy recommendations of the communications elites.

Types of Foreign Policy Elites

The elite groups which share in the process of policy initiation and formation may be classified functionally under four main headings.

1. The *political elites* which include the publicly elected, high appointive, as well as the party leaders. The official political elite, of course, is subdivided according to its position in the policy-making process (i.e., legislative, executive,

judicial) and according to the policy subject matter with which it is charged (e.g., in the foreign policy field, the Department of State and the foreign affairs committees of the House and Senate).

2. The *administrative* or *bureaucratic elites* which include the professional corps of the executive establishment who enjoy special powers by virtue of their interest in and familiarity and immediate contact with particular policy problems.

3. The *interest elites* which include the representatives of the vast number of private, policy-oriented associations, ranging from huge nation-wide aggregations to local formations and organized around aims and objectives which in their variety reflect the economic, ethnic, religious, and ideological complexity of the American population. Here too, as with the *political elites,* we may distinguish between the *elected* or *political interest elites* and the *bureaucratic staffs* which have an importance in the field of interest group activity comparable to that of the governmental bureaucracy in official policy-making. They too are on the daily firing line of decision-making and enjoy powers in practice which are not formally recognized in the legal distribution of authority.

4. Finally, there are the *communications elites,* the most obvious representatives of which are the owners, controllers, and active participants of the mass media—radio, press, and movies. Careful analysis, however, indicates that the swift development and prominence of the mass media have tended to obscure the continued decisive importance of more intimate forms of communication in the shaping of popular attitudes.[5] Perhaps the most effective opinion leaders are the vast number of vocational, community, and institutional "notables," known and trusted men and women—clergy-

men and influential lay churchmen, club and fraternal order leaders, teachers and the like—with personal followings. It may even be said that mass communication becomes more effective in the degree that it approximates the more intimate relationship between a personally known leader and his following. Thus, the "fireside chat," and the favorite columnist almost succeed in dissociating themselves from the impersonality and superficial impact of the mass media.

Any simple description of the structure of communications necessarily does violence to its variety and complexity. It overlaps with the political, bureaucratic, and interest group elites—all of whom compete for the attention of various publics via the media of communication. In this classification, however, the communications elites are limited to the *specialists* in communication—newspapermen, radio and movie personnel, teachers, clergymen, publicists, and the like.

Another method of elite classification might be based on policy interests and specializations. Thus one might speak of the foreign policy elite as having a political sector including the elected officials and their advisers especially charged with foreign policy decisions, the bureaucratic sector which includes the professional administrative personnel in and outside the State Department who deal with foreign policy questions, the interest group sector which includes the leadership of "foreign policy associations" as well as the foreign policy specialists within the more general interest organizations, and finally the communications sector which includes among others, publishers, editors, journalists, publicists, commentators, and teachers who are partly, primarily, or entirely devoted to foreign policy problems.

These various elites have quite different relationships with their followings. In some cases the system of selection facilitates intra-elite competition and rank-and-file control; in others, popular control and competition are minimized. Also, the degree to which publics are interested in "controlling" the policy decisions of their leadership varies with the nature of the issue and the pressures of the time.

All of these factors combine to reduce popular control to the status of a crude and primarily passive instrument. But this does not by any means suggest that its role in policy-making is insignificant. The various policy and opinion elites are continually, and more or less freely, recruited from the rank and file and consequently share in its prejudices and preferences. In addition they compete with one another in the "opinion markets" for the "sale" of policies. In most cases the influential policy alternatives placed before the public, or its constituent parts, represent in more or less articulate form the vaguer impulses and preferences of the masses.

But even this degree of popular control over the opinion and policy leaderships presupposes a measure of interest in, and awareness of, the issues on the part of the public. An obvious principle may be advanced in this connection that the influence of elite and minority groups in policy-making varies with the level of public concern with the issue. There are situations in which public predispositions set up a stony resistance to all appeals for change—widespread preferences or prejudices on which the hopes of propagandists are repeatedly crushed. There are other situations in which significant decisions fail to activate recognition or emotion among the public, and in which a free channel of decision is accorded to interested groups. It can hardly be said that these moods of public interest and apathy follow any rational pattern. For an issue which is met with indifference today may tomorrow provoke grave public concern. In this connection, a second principle may be hazarded that the public does not see the interdependence of decisions and policies. Only those aspects of the policy-making process really impinge on the public which directly involve immediate and observable interests.

The converse of this principle has a special bearing on the problem of public opinion and foreign policy. In the degree to which issues and decisions are remote, the incapacity of the public to grasp the issues and its consequent indifference accords a special importance to the initiatives and pressures of interested elite and minority groups. Under circumstances of peace or of only moderate international tension, most of the daily decisions of diplomacy and foreign policy are "remote." They involve little known peoples in far-away countries, or highly technical problems such as boundary settlements, international trade, and the complex issues of foreign loans and foreign economies. They are, indeed, the stuff out of which war and peace, victory and defeat, are made. But foreign policy is a tapestry of infinite complexity, and even the expert can only hope to achieve familiarity with a part of its intricate designs.

The American and Soviet Elites

There are at least three points of essential difference between the Soviet and American elites. In the United States there is both a public and private separation of powers as well as a specialization of functions. This is not only a case where executive, legislature, and judiciary can bind one another only with great difficulty, but also one in which the interest groups and communications elites are autonomous as functional groupings and as individual units. Policy unity in the public and private sectors can only be produced by *voluntary co-ordination.* There is no single point in the policy-making process where the strings of influence, so to speak, are held in a single hand. In this sense the Soviet elite is *functionally co-ordinated;* there is a comparatively clear chain of command which mobilizes all the significant policy and opinion functions and points of influence.

A second significant difference has to do with the nature of elite *controls* over the rank and file of the population. In the United States this relationship is one of contingency, enforced by electoral processes or by the conditions of a relatively competitive opinion and policy market. In the Soviet Union the relationship is one of *command* and of elite selection from the top down, enforced by a monopoly of coercion and manipulation.

A third significant difference has to do with the ideological composition of the American and Soviet elites. The American elites are *ideologically heterogeneous,* that is to say they differ significantly among themselves with regard both to the means and ends of policy. A common policy can only be produced on the basis of an *ideological consensus.* In contrast among the Communist cadres there is a continual process of ideological and policy purification. Ideological conformity among the elites is *compulsive* and not consensual.

Among the many problems created by these peculiar attributes of the American elite a few call for special comment. Thus the functional autonomy of the American elites produces a situation of uncertainty with regard to the initiative in policy-making. In a formal sense the assumption is that the executive takes the initiative in the making of foreign policy, but his actions are constantly influenced by his calculations as to the reactions of this or that elite—Congress, the press, the trade-union leadership, and the like. At the minimum, such an elite structure produces remediable delays; but there are situations when serious losses result, when a vicious circle of elite irresponsibility [6] sets in and precious opportunities are lost, or precious assets are wasted. Such a situation tends to encourage defensive improvisation in policy and to discourage far-sighted policy enterprise.

A second problem is elite unpredictability which produces policy instability and inconsistency. These tendencies arise out of the autonomy of the various sectors of the elite, combined with ideological differences which lead people to start from different premises and to stress different factors in policy situations. There is indeed a certain flexibility, a certain experimentalism in such a structure, a capacity to shift quickly from one policy to another. At the same time it has created the stereotype of American unreliability and instability in foreign policy. That this tendency can be disciplined in situations of dramatic threat has been demonstrated in the foreign policy developments of the past years. But it is useful to remember that it is the type of weakness which is more characteristically reflected in periods of foreign policy "normalcy." Under such conditions of relaxation the functional autonomy and ideological heterogeneity of the elites may produce a flowering of mutually incompatible reactions and policies, and under some circumstances an incapacity for making any policy at all.

A third difficulty might be described as the problem of "elite depth." Here we touch on one of the essential criteria of a democratic foreign policy. A democratic foreign policy in the realistic sense of that term has to involve broad discussion among the elites before the attentive public. Communist foreign policy acquires its stability by being derived from an explicit social theory authoritatively interpreted at a single political point. American foreign policy acquires strength to the extent that it is derived from competitive discussion in front of a critical audience capable of judgment and discrimination. Thus limitations in knowledge on particular geographical regions, or failures to recognize the possibilities and limitations of the various instruments of foreign policy may seriously affect the quality of foreign policy discussion and result in grave security risks and losses. An obvious illustration is the difference in the quality of American foreign policy in the Western Hemisphere and Western Europe, as compared with our policies in the Eastern cultural regions. An informed elite, both public and private, and a large attentive audience have produced a Western European policy of considerable discrimination and effectiveness. Erroneous policies from the point of view of American security interests (such as the Morgenthau Plan) could be corrected because an active competitive discussion was possible. When we leave the Western Hemisphere and Western Europe, we are leaving the areas with which we have binding cultural ties and a common network of communication, for cultures which few of us understand. The number of persons in the United States capable of critical evaluation of a policy for the Far East or the Middle East is extremely small. Consequently, competitive elite discussion is possible only to a limited degree, and enormous power gravitates to the few experts. A bias among the experts can, and often does, go uncorrected. The peculiar strengths of democratic policy-making are not applicable in a situation where knowledge and insight is confined to a shallow and restricted sector of the policy and opinion elites.

This problem of depth and variety of discussion does not only apply to regional and cultural attention biases, but also to failures to grasp the values and possibilities of the various instruments of foreign policy. This brings us to a fourth weakness in the American foreign policy elite. How can we counteract the extreme tendencies toward specialization in American culture—tendencies which produce military, diplomatic, economic, and propaganda virtuosi, but which fail to produce leaders capable of integrating all the means of foreign policy and placing them in the service of American aims. There are no points in American culture where such leaders are trained and no established channels of recruitment whereby their access to influence may be facilitated. In this regard the Soviet elites have certain obvious advantages. Leninist-Stalinist Communism is pre-eminently a training school for political virtuosi. The top Communist elites may be thought of as theater commanders with an explicit set of objectives and an understanding of the values of, and relations between, the various branches of political warfare. They combine the skills of propaganda, military strategy and tactics, diplomacy, and economics in a single homogeneous leadership corps. A Communist Politburo approximates the role of the conductor of a well-trained orchestra in which the competing claims of the instrument types are co-ordinated. This of course is without regard to the quality of the political music produced or the extent to which the values of the instruments are appreciated. The American policy orchestra is one in which the instrumental specializations tend to follow their own bents—the brass (to say nothing of the various brass sections) strive to fulfill the values of brass, while the woodwinds, strings, and percussion pursue their own musical missions. This is not to argue in favor of an authoritarian policy conductor but only to raise the crucial question of how the United States can recruit and utilize the political virtuosi which it so urgently requires. There is a heritage of Jacksonian amateurism which perpetuates the myth that America is full of Cincinnatuses, who in the extremity of their country's need can drop their tractors, typewriters, and assembly lines, and lead us against the modern Aequi, out of the valley of the Algidus.

What is called for at the policy level is an explicit interpretation of American aims and objectives, plus an eclectic and flexible appreciation of the suitability of the various means of policy. In contrast, the stratification of American society, the specialization of elite functions, and the over-all cultural atmosphere of competitiveness have produced among the elites biases of interest, perspective and technique. These biases represented a more or less effective adjustment to the political situation of the prewar period. They are even today more or less effective adjustments to the conditions of domestic political competition. Thus a hard advocacy of special interest is part of the political bargaining game in the United States. But a totally new world political situation has emerged since World War II which raises serious questions about the consequences of patterns of this kind for our national security.

Most elite members are skilled organizers, propagandists, or manipulators who restrict their rational critical powers to the consideration of the means to implement policies or values which result from their interest positions. Similarly, most elite members demonstrate means biases. Thus if we place a journalist in a responsible position in the field of foreign propaganda policy he is typically limited to American journalistic methods and premises. There are within the American elites rigidities in value and policy, and rigidities in the approach to political techniques which significantly influence the content of elite foreign policy proposals.

The statesman, as an American cultural ideal, is the man who has overcome these narrow rigidities of interest and method: he is capable of taking the "long view" and the "technically effective" view. The selection and training of elites in the United States and the circumstances of their adult careers hardly facilitate the development of this analytical and integrative mentality. There is an anti-intellectual bias not only among the masses of the population but among the elites as well. The cultural pressure toward improvisation and gadgetry, the optimistic faith that the world owes Americans a simple solution to their problems reaches high in the influential strata. Similarly, though policy-thinking at the elite level has more intellectual structure and factual content, it shares with mass thinking the instability of moods and simplifications of political reality.

If we look at American politicians from whose ranks come presidents, cabinet members, and congressmen we find a predominating spirit of brokerage. The function of the American politician is to find the terms on the basis of which conflicting social groups will live together peacefully. He is, according to Pendleton Herring, a "specialist in human relations." [7] But his special talents are intuitive in character and local in application. He operates by feel in a situation with which he is intimately familiar. Like most persons lacking experience with foreign cultures or comparable formal training, he tends to project on foreign cultures and elites his own premises and expectations. Perhaps nothing illustrates this so well as the assumptions of American foreign policy in the "honeymoon phase" of Soviet-American relations. Men like Roosevelt and Byrnes apparently continued to hope, even after they had ceased to expect, that the Soviet elites would react "like Americans" to offers of compromise.

The professional foreign policy bureaucracy is better prepared in this regard, but here too, persons of ambassadorial or ministerial rank and non-State Department personnel on foreign missions often show this same parochial and projective mentality. They often operate with Frenchmen, Italians, and even Chinese with the expectation that they will respond to American incentives and according to American codes of behavior.[8] The recognition of the research and the policy-planning function in the State Department is a recent one. The relation of propaganda to foreign policy is only dimly understood, and as a consequence it is poorly integrated with the other instruments of foreign policy. The professional foreign service officers, while possessing discipline and an essential *esprit de corps*, have only recently come to recognize the complexities of foreign policy making, and the importance of the research and the policy-planning function.

Among the "private" elites the situation is even more problematical. The various foreign policy associations and civic organizations which operate on a quite high level of information and critical discrimination, play an important role within the limited "attentive public." These private agencies are of significance in creating "audience depth" for elite foreign policy discussion.

But until recently most of the great interest groups approached foreign policy problems with little if any professional advice. The approach to foreign policy represented a mere extension of domestic interests into the foreign sphere. As illustrations we might cite the historic position of business, labor, and agricultural groups on such questions as the tariff, the position of business organizations on the protection of investments abroad, the position of organized labor on immigration problems, the position of veterans' organizations on the national defense. World War II and the postwar crisis have broken into this historic pressure group parochialism and have stimulated broader conceptions of foreign policy problems. Many of the great pressure groups now have staffs which specialize in foreign policy problems. But this broader view has hardly penetrated into the leading echelons of the pressure groups. Here a narrow interest mentality continues to prevail among most organizations.[9] While there is some recognition in the present crisis that interest advocacy cannot be pressed with the same freedom in foreign policy matters as in domestic, this falls far short of a creative and flexible approach. The pressure group bureaucracies, with a few exceptions, adhere to a broad national and humanitarian foreign policy in principle, but undermine it in practice when hard, tangible interests are involved. The experience of the Economic Co-operation Administration with such pressures for special treatment of agricultural and business interests is only the most recent illustration of this type of lip-devotion.

It is unrealistic to expect anything more from this quarter than an increasingly enlightened interest representation. This may be approximated by increasing inclusion of foreign policy specialists on the staffs of pressure groups and allowing to such individuals fairly wide discretion in proposing adjustments of the special interest to the general. This may produce interest-group statesmanship, but not national statesmanship.

Greater hopes might be entertained for the communications elites which claim the function of informing and educating. But if we turn to the mass media, and particularly those enterprises which reach large publics, we encounter interest bias, sensationalism, or the assertion of a formal neutrality on controversial policy problems. ". . . the press emphasizes the exceptional rather than the representative, the sensational rather than the significant."[10] The few newspapers and columnists that adhere to a higher standard have only a small readership among the "attentive" public. The mass media tend to accentuate crisis and deepen complacency; in general, they play up to the mood susceptibilities of the mass audience.

The radio and the movies are primarily vehicles of entertainment. The news function of radio is on the whole satisfactorily performed, but there is little of the essential interpretation of the "background" to give the listener a sense of the meaning of events. ". . . about 40 per cent of the people of America got, in 1946, what was described as commentary at the rate of two hours a week, half of it outside the best listening periods, 90 per cent of it supplied by 'commentators' who lacked even the minimal qualifications for such work." [11] The cinema (at least that part of it which reaches large audiences) is almost entirely a vehicle of entertainment. Its role in the development of mature attitudes toward problems of foreign policy is primarily indirect, but nevertheless important. The function of entertainment is to divert attention, to provide imaginary escapes from the tedium of the everyday, to offer targets for the discharge of hostilities and wants which cannot otherwise be safely or readily discharged. The function of art encompasses these essential purposes, but goes beyond them by providing what, for lack of a better term, might be called a "moral lift," a refinement of emotion, a greater and more humane perspective, a delivery from the crampedness of the self. As the great vehicle of mass art, the movies in the United States have tended to restrict their efforts to entertainment. They have adapted themselves with great skill to the standards of the huge audiences which their economic structure requires. They have refused to accept the risks of subtlety and experimentalism, except in the technical sense. Most movie plots are skillfully directed toward, and tend to perpetuate, those qualities of character which have already been treated at an earlier point. Some evidence is forthcoming at the present time that the film industry will experiment with, and the public attend, movies which admit the possibility of tragedy and frustration. But at the moment these are still rare deviations.[12]

The religious and educational leaderships are among the most important in the sphere of primary communications. In so far as they have established relations of confidence with their followings, they act in an atmosphere of trust and intimacy which opens minds to new insights. It is no more than an impressionistic conclusion to suggest that they rarely provide the kind of moral and intellectual guidance which develops realistic and analytical habits of thought. If the pressure group elites sit on the cynical horn of the American dilemma, the religious and educational elites sit on the idealistic one. Both tend to perpetuate the moral dualism which confuses efforts at rational policy-making. The brand of idealism proposed is in most cases so obviously in conflict with what is realistically possible that it cannot serve as a guide to conduct. As we shall have the occasion to observe at a later point, the religious elites tend to view security values and coercive means with something less than the directness and resolution which seems to be required.

The social scientist in institutions of higher learning often lays claim to a wide mandate to criticize the flow of policy as it passes before his vision. His powers are indeed impressive. Practically the whole of the younger elite generation is subject to his influence—future politicians, diplomats, journalists, columnists, clergymen, teachers, trade-union and interest association leaders. And in his capacity as scholar and expert he has a direct channel to public opinion and policy-making. Yet the evidence suggests that these magnificent opportunities for social influence are hardly recognized, and even more rarely utilized, by the great bulk of the academic profession. In most of the social sciences the level of analysis and of theory is so low that techniques can masquerade as disciplines, and parts represent themselves as wholes. Only a small number of students, and these mainly by their own efforts, emerge from this training with an understanding of the interrelatedness of social processes and a capacity for policy analysis.[13]

When we examine the current scholarly output of political science (which makes claims of being expert in the field of foreign policy) the shortcomings of at least this sector of the academic elite become disturbingly clear. Such an evaluation has to proceed from acceptable criteria [14] as to what types of knowledge and methods are required for the development of a capacity to understand foreign policy issues and to make intelligent foreign policy proposals. Such criteria would include:

(1) A conscious awareness of the essential value conflicts underlying foreign policy controversies. This rests upon knowledge of the basic socio-psychological, cultural, ideological, and legal-constitutional factors affecting the policies of significant nations and regions;

(2) an expertness in the special procedures, institutions, and problems of international relations;

(3) an understanding of the role and limitations of the various instrumentalities or means of foreign policy —military, diplomatic, economic, and ideological.

If we examine the contribution of political science it is evident that this sector of elite training and recruitment falls far short of its mission.[15] Judging by published articles in the general political science journals since the end of the war, we conclude that the political scientist has primarily played the role of providing the historical and descriptive background on foreign governments and politics, foreign and international legal institutions, and foreign ideologies. Fifty-four per cent of the articles on foreign affairs dealt with these traditional fields of political science. Another 14 per cent dealt with the foreign policies of particular countries again primarily in expository or historical terms.

A number of significant blind spots in subject matter come to light in this topical analysis of recent publications. First, there were no articles on American politics as it affected foreign policy and international relations. Second, there were only a small number (6 per cent) of articles treating the political aspects of military security problems. Third, very little attention was paid to the role of economic and socio-cultural factors affecting international relations.

There can be little question but that political scientists are becoming increasingly aware of the importance of these basic economic and social factors which underlie policy problems in international relations. But there is still little evidence to show that political science training and research has begun to assimilate these new insights and approaches.

Study of the methods employed in political science research of the postwar period also reflected significant shortcomings. Not only was the subject matter still limited to the traditional conceptions of political science, but the methods were primarily historical and descriptive. Fifty-two per cent of the articles were straightforward historical, descriptive, or expository treatments of government, law, politics, and political ideas. Most of the remainder contained analysis in a quite subordinate relationship to historical and descriptive treatment. Much of the primarily analytical material was legal analysis, or analysis of the characteristics and consequences of particular types of governmental institutions. The systematic analysis of policy alternatives, or the analysis of basic social, psychological, and economic factors as they apply to policy problems, was definitely a very minor theme among political scientists.

If these trends reflect the pedagogy and public influence of political science, then it can fairly be concluded that the political scientist leaves largely to his student and lay audience the important task of evaluating policy alternatives. These shortcomings have serious consequences for the development of statesmanship in America. The social sciences in the modern university constitute a kind of throat through which the future elite generations pass. This is the only formal opportunity for intensive training in the bases and means of policy-making. An enormous opportunity for constructive social influence is being exploited halfheartedly or not at all.

These criticisms of the discipline of political science should not by implication suggest that the newer social science approaches, such as social psychology and anthropology, turn in a better performance from the point of view of our criteria. They have developed methods of the first importance and have been enormously productive of insights and hypotheses. But many of their practitioners are simple amateurs and often pretentious ones when it comes to proposals applicable to problems of foreign policy. If these newer disciplines wish to deliver on their claims to policy relevance, they have to recognize that they have but a piece of the picture and that they cannot fully grasp the potentialities and limitations of their own contributions until they become aware of the contributions and methods of their neighboring disciplines.

It is, of course, clear that the particular combination of

skills and qualities of character under discussion cannot in any direct sense be deliberately planned and produced by schools or any other formal means of selection. Politics is an art; and statesmanship is its highest flowering. In final analysis, the emergence of men with responsible political callings is never predictable, but always accidental. However, it is possible to facilitate the selection of such types and to provide them with the tools and wisdom of their vocation. It is in this regard that the social sciences have an enormous opportunity. For they receive the elite cadres at points in their development when there is still a certain flexibility and openness, a receptivity to challenging ideals and images.

To the practitioner of the social science discipline who meets this criticism with the argument that man has but a short life and that such a challenge is beyond the capacity of ordinary flesh, there is but one answer. If he claims for his work a relevance to the solution of crucial policy problems, he can no longer hide behind the barriers of a single discipline. The crisis of our time has in a mere decade created an enormous scientific obsolescence. The academic elites, so often prone to trumpeting moral challenges to politicians and laymen, are confronted by a historic challenge all their own.

The recruitment and training of a policy and opinion elite capable of performing the grave tasks of modern foreign policy have therefore to be recognized as largely "new business" on the American agenda. It is in this area, rather than in mass information programs, that the most may be accomplished with the least expenditure of resources. The broad consensus of foreign policy which obtains at the present time is a product of well-dramatized, external threat. We have to strive for a type of democratic elite discipline which is proof against the transient shifts of political atmosphere and foreign policy moods.

VIII. The Foreign Policy Consensus

WHILE the policy disunity and conflicts of the American elites are in sharp contrast to the compulsive ideological homogeneity of the Communist elites, there is, nevertheless, a general ideological consensus in the United States in which the mass of the population and its leadership generally share. At the level of basic attitudes this is largely an unconscious consensus of feeling with regard to values and of reactions regarded as suitable in response to certain political cues. There are underlying assumptions as to the inherent propriety of such values as mass material welfare and freedom and of certain modes of resolving political differences. At the level of general opinion on public policy, one may speak of a consensus of mood, of shared emotional states in response to changes in the domestic and foreign arenas. At the level of articulate elite policy formulation there is a broad consensus of policy. Neither in foreign nor in domestic policy is this to be understood as full agreement on principles or on details, but rather as an adherence to a broad compromise on political procedures and policies. Such adherence ranges from unqualified enthusiasm to a mere readiness to tolerate.

The foreign policy consensus is full of unilateral reservations, special emphases, and actual and potential conflicts of both an ideological and an interest character. Furthermore, the breadth and solidity of this consensus must be understood as having been produced by the circumstance of an external crisis combined with a fairly satisfactory internal situation. How stable this consensus is likely to be under other circumstances is discussed at a later point.

What distinguishes the foreign policy consensus from the deviational foreign policy positions discussed in the following chapter is agreement on the main themes of contemporary foreign policy—resistance to Communist expansion by economic, diplomatic, propaganda, and, if necessary, military means, and the establishment of a peaceful and legal international order in which American material and security interests would be protected. More basically, this foreign policy consensus is founded upon a consensus of fundamental attitudes and ideology which may be described in two dimensions—values and means. The advocates of the American foreign policy consensus are, in general, agreed that the primary aims of American policy, both domestic and foreign, should turn on a reconciliation of individual freedom and mass welfare of a primarily material kind. This is a broad substratum of agreement on which such divergent groups as Republicans and Democrats, laborites and capitalists, and the various cultural, regional, and religious groupings take a common stand, even though this agreement is obscured at the level of overt policy by the clamor and demagogy of special interest representation. The foreign policy consensus is also characterized by a basic agreement on means. There is a kind of rational eclecticism as to means; there is no rejection of coercion as such or of security diplomacy based on the threat of coercion, as is the case with such deviational groups as pacifists and certain of the internationalists. As a type of social action the foreign policy consensus approximates Max Weber's "instrumental rationality." Attitudes toward ends and means are contingent rather than absolute. In contrast, the foreign policy counter-elites discussed in the next chapter approximate the type of "absolute value rationality," in rejecting unconditionally certain policy ends or means and asserting certain others in a rigid manner.[1]

The Foreign Policies of the Labor Organizations

The great labor organizations of the United States—the American Federation of Labor and the Congress of Industrial Organizations—in most respects support the present American foreign policy. But the CIO has been slower than the AFL to adopt the current position. In the fall of 1947, after the enactment of the Greek-Turkish aid bill and during the Marshall Plan debate, the CIO adopted a "warmongering" resolution reminiscent of Vyshinsky's famous speech in the earlier part of the year. The CIO gave qualified support of the Marshall Plan, still in the hope that the program would not be limited to the non-Communist countries. The CIO also took a position in opposition to any form of compulsory military service—both universal military training and selective service.[2] It was notable that the foreign policy resolutions of the 1947 convention were supported by both Communists and anti-Communists. After the convention the CIO came out in specific approval of the European Recovery Program. It was during 1948 that the CIO leadership checked the influence of the Communist minority in its ranks and came to the support of administration policy on the threat of Communism.

The CIO foreign policy resolution of 1948 condemned the Soviet Union's use of the veto in the Security Council and its destruction of the independence of the Iron Curtain countries. It specifically condemned the Berlin blockade and reaffirmed its support of the European Recovery Program. Subsequently the CIO Executive Board came out in full support of the North Atlantic Pact.[3]

The 1948 shift in CIO policy was adopted over the sharp protests of such Communist union delegations as those of the electrical workers, the communications workers, and the fur and leather workers.[4] In addition, there were internal struggles within some of the constituent unions with strong Communist minorities. The foreign policy shift of the CIO has been accompanied by CIO efforts to purge its leading cadres of Communists.

Though the CIO now shares in the foreign policy consensus it is critical of certain specific policies. This is especially true of occupation policy in Germany and Japan. It has specifically attacked the military government trade-union policy in Germany for its neutrality, urging that the government should offer outright assistance to the German labor movement. It has also attacked the American denazification and decartelization program as having been weakly enforced. The CIO has taken a similar position with regard to policy in Japan which it describes as oppressive of Japanese trade-unionism. It advocated the strengthening of civilian and particularly labor influences in the MacArthur administration.[5]

In general the CIO has adopted the administration policy with left overtones. It frequently finds itself in sympathy with the European socialists and left Catholics by virtue of the influence of liberal Catholics and moderate Socialists in its own ranks.

Not troubled by a powerful Communist faction, the AFL accepted the general American view of the threat of Communism sooner than the CIO. In its 1947 Convention the AFL sharply criticized the policy of the Soviet Union and approved the program of Greek-Turkish aid and the Marshall Plan.[6] Its policy with regard to military service was less sweeping than that of the CIO. While it opposed universal military training it favored a limited form of selective service. Like the CIO, it offers unqualified support to the North Atlantic Pact. It is also in agreement with the CIO in imputing a conservative and an anti–trade-union bias to American occupation policy in Germany and Japan.[7] Both the CIO and the AFL maintain observers in Germany and Japan and have representatives on the staff of the Economic Co-operation Administration. Both unions share in an effort to bring American foreign policy to the support of the trade-union and moderate left elements abroad.

The AFL deviates most markedly from the CIO and from administration foreign policy in its position on foreign trade. The older trade-union organization is still influenced by its earlier policy of protectionism. In its 1948 Convention it qualified its approval of the Reciprocal Trade Agreements Act by the statement that "in some instances the duty reductions already made have reached the point where further reductions would endanger the employment in particular industries exposed to competition from abroad." [8] In his testimony as President of the American Wage Earners Protective Conference (tariff group of the AFL) before a Congressional Committee, Matthew Woll urged that the renewal of the Reciprocal Trade Agreements Act contain "a limitation . . . providing that competitive imports of workers in foreign countries be denied entry in American markets at total landed costs, tariff duties paid, which are less than American costs of production and wholesale ceiling prices of products of American workers when such competitive products are commercially available." [9] While the general CIO position on reciprocal trade is one of unqualified support, at least one of its constituent organizations—

that of the Textile Workers Union of America—takes a stand similar to that of Matthew Woll of the AFL. Emil Rieve, president of the Textile Workers, expressed general approval of the spirit of the Reciprocal Trade Agreements Act, but stated in conclusion: "On an over-all basis it appears that further reductions in tariff rates for textile products are not seriously feasible." [10]

Deviations within the foreign policy consensus can take the form of ideological or special interest dissent. In this sense, the equivocal position of the CIO in 1947 represented an ideological equivocation resulting from the pressure of the "radical appeasement" groups within its own organization. At the present time both the AFL and the CIO present a special ideological emphasis within the foreign policy consensus in favor of pro–trade-union and welfare policies both at home and abroad. This does not place the trade-unions in the present context outside of the foreign policy consensus since the ideology of American foreign policy includes these moderate left aims. The American trade-unions have appointed themselves the guardians of this particular foreign policy value. The AFL position on reciprocal trade is an illustration of a special interest deviation, a difference not in explicit ideology, but rather to be understood as a policy inconsistency. Matthew Woll and his followers find it possible to advocate a general policy of economic and political internationalism, and at the same time a specific policy of economic nationalism.

The Foreign Policies of Business Organizations

The United States Chamber of Commerce is the largest and most representative organization of business men in the country. It is of interest, therefore, that it has fully supported administration foreign policy since the end of the war on military, economic, and diplomatic questions. On issues involving economic questions it has moderately urged the desirability of preserving and expanding the free-enterprise system both in the United States and abroad. In this regard the Chamber of Commerce and other business organizations have played at the other end of the keyboard from the labor organizations. But "business bias" has never taken the form of a deviation in principle from significant "bipartisan" policies.

In the field of foreign trade the Chamber of Commerce has approved the extension of the Reciprocal Trade Agreements Act with the proviso, "Neither in the original form nor in practical application by reason of events that were not contemplated should agreements be permitted to cause destructive competition in American agriculture or industry." [11] Despite this assertion of protectionism the Chamber approved the extension of the Act for three years without amendment.

Its support of the Marshall Plan was qualified only by insistence on "sound economic principles" and "businesslike methods." It recommended that the program of "aid for economic improvement should be, insofar as possible, direct from industry to industry rather than from government to government." [12] But here again its "free enterprise" emphasis did not result in a conditional approval. In contrast to the National Association of Manufacturers, the Chamber explicitly disapproved any policy of imposing political restrictions on American aid.

"The U.S. is not interested in imposing its political or social system on any country or region in the world. Conversely it is determined that no other nation shall impose its system or ideology on ours. Consequently, whatever the political ideology of the recipient nations, or their manifestation in practice, so long as the essential human freedoms, as set forth in our Bill of Rights, are preserved, the United States of America should carry out its commitments under any aid program agreed upon." [13]

In the field of national security the Chamber has approved universal military training and the use of selective service when necessary; it supported the Greek-Turkish aid program and the North Atlantic Pact, arguing that these security measures have been necessary because of the blocking of effective United Nations action by the Soviet Union.

The United States Junior Chamber of Commerce, a national organization of young businessmen below the age of thirty-five, takes a position quite similar to that of the Chamber of Commerce proper. At the same time it is characterized by a much stronger current of free-enterprise evangelism and international idealism. It has urged a program of strenuous propaganda for free enterprise abroad. Thus in its ERP testimony one of its leaders stated:

"With each grain of wheat and copper penny, we should send as a companion of equal dignity and importance a dose of the old fashioned gospel of democracy—pointing out that only under our system of free opportunity and enterprise has a people been able to work and produce enough to relieve the chaos of a troubled world. This is no time for false modesty. The scream of the American Eagle must be heard around the world . . ." [14]

The Junior Chamber has been greatly influenced by world government proposals. It advocates the abolition of the veto power in the Security Council, the granting of power to legislate and tax to the world organization, and the granting of compulsory jurisdiction to the International Court of Justice in disputes which cannot be resolved in the Security Council or the General Assembly of the United Nations.[15] This evangelist and idealist trend in the Junior Chamber conforms to the pattern of foreign policy attitudes of youth reported in the previous chapter.

The Committee for Economic Development is the spokesman for the liberal sector of American business. At the present time it is not a mass membership organization; it is a national committee of interested businessmen who subsidize and sponsor research mainly directed toward moderating the fluctuations of the business cycle. The foreign policy proposals of the Committee reflect the least amount of "business bias" of any of the business organizations. Its approval of the Trade Agreements Act was without qualification except that it "should be pressed vigorously so as to bring about substantial rate reductions."[16] In later statements the CED has defended the full free trade position, arguing that "American industry [in a free trade system] will work toward a more productive pattern by stimulating the expansion of those industries in which American labor and management are most productive. We shall receive more abundantly those goods and services from other countries which are superior to our own in quality, design and price."[17] The CED position on European aid was greatly influenced by Paul Hoffman who later became the administrator of the Economic Co-operation Administration. This position was one of full approval of the Marshall Plan idea. The organization went into great detail in specifying the policies and form of administration most likely to accomplish American foreign policy aims.[18] In many respects these proposals have been carried out in the policies and procedures of the present Economic Co-operation Administration.

As guardian of the right-wing version of American business ideology, the National Association of Manufacturers has been subject to increasingly sharp criticism from within the business community itself. Its almost complete negativism in social policy has greatly reduced its influence on legislation and has provoked a serious internal struggle within its leadership. But the "liberal wing" within the NAM has not succeeded in breaking the hold of the old-line leadership and bureaucracy. Its main achievement thus far has been to provide an increasingly effective opposition to the organization's still dominant reactionary policy.[19]

The foreign policy of the NAM falls partly in and partly outside of the foreign policy consensus. In its attitudes on questions of national defense and security policy it has been fully in support of administration policy. It has strongly favored universal military training, selective service, and the building of stockpiles of strategic defense materials. But in its position on the tariff and European aid its position has been a nationalist one both economically and ideologically. Thus on the extension of the Reciprocal Trade Agreements Act the NAM approved extension for one year only. It recommended further amendments which would have seriously restricted the functioning of the law even during this limited period. "In view of the economic uncertainties . . . we strongly advise against any general numerical increase in reciprocal agreements during the ensuing year. . . . There should be eliminated from the present bill the provision which would enlarge the power to change tariff rates in reciprocal trade agreements." [20]

The ideological nationalism of the NAM is reflected in its position on the European Recovery Program. Over the protests of a small but vigorous minority it urged "that during the period of economic aid the participating nations should not undertake any further nationalization projects, or initiate projects which have the effect of destroying or impairing private competitive enterprise, and thus retard their economic progress." [21] Such a position meant, in effect if not in intent, a rejection of the Marshall Plan itself, since such gross intervention in the internal affairs of foreign countries would probably have provoked a collapse of the entire project.

The Foreign Policies of Agricultural Organizations

The larger farm organizations present a far more complex and heterogeneous ideological picture than those of labor and business. Traditional conceptions among the rural population are more likely to persist despite dramatic political, social, and military changes. In this regard the articulate policies of the pressure groups of agriculture confirm the findings of public opinion research as to the greater traditionalism of the rural population. This traditionalism is shown in the stability of attitude of radical, as well as conservative, agrarianism.

There are three leading agricultural pressure groups. The largest organization—the American Farm Bureau Federation—holds to a moderate central position; the National Grange on the right holds a position of economic nationalism and moral conservatism; and the National Farmers Union on the left perpetuates the peculiar radical agrarian combination of isolationism and pacifist internationalism.

The Farm Bureau has accepted the bipartisan foreign policy in almost every respect. In defense and security matters it has approved of selective service, Greek-Turkish aid, and the North Atlantic Pact. In matters of foreign economic policy it gave unqualified approval to the expansion of the Reciprocal Trade program and the International Trade Organization. Similarly its approval of the European Recovery Program was unqualified. It opposed a policy of dumping agricultural surpluses under the Economic Cooperation Administration. "To the extent surpluses can be utilized to contribute to recovery they should be used. However, the United States should avoid using this program to force its surpluses on participating nations at the expense of other items which would contribute more to recovery." [22]

The position of the National Grange is an interesting combination of moderate pacifist internationalism and economic nationalism. In both respects it falls half in and half out of the foreign policy consensus. The Grange has opposed universal military training and selective service, claiming that voluntary enlistment is a sufficient source of military manpower in times of peace. Only in an actual war crisis should selective service be resorted to. [23] The Grange has also advocated the reform of the United Nations in the direction of making the General Assembly a legislative body "provided that some practical and equitable system of weighted representation can be developed." [24]

The deviation of the Grange from the foreign policy consensus is more explicit in the field of foreign economic policy. It specifically opposed the extension of the Reciprocal Trade Agreements Act. "America needs a tariff policy designed to protect agriculture, labor and industry from competition based on conscripted labor or low standards of living. . . . We would prefer to see the Reciprocal

Trade Agreements Act expire than to see it renewed in its present form." [25]

The National Grange has approved the Marshall Plan after a period of doubt. It at first insisted that aid ought to take the form of loans only and not grants, a reflection, perhaps, of outraged rural frugalism over "billion-dollar handouts." It subsequently changed its position in favor of the act. Interestingly enough in coming out for the act, the Grange representative moved to the other extreme, reflecting the American tendency to fluctuate from "hard-headedness" to idealism commented on at an earlier point. He urged that the program of aid should not be used in any way to influence political developments in Western Europe. "We should defend the right of any people to freely choose by democratic means the type of government they want, whether that be democracy, communism, or dictatorship." He would only object to Communism *if* it attempted to impose its scheme of government and ideology on other countries.[26]

This strain of pacifist and international idealism (unsullied by economic nationalism) is to be found with far more clarity in the National Farmers Union,[27] the contemporary bearer of historic midwestern agrarian radicalism. What is of particular interest in the position of the Farmers Union is that it couples an almost unqualified internationalism with an underlying distrust of "foreign power politics," an attitude which leads it into an isolationist position. One may arrive at an isolationist position along more than one avenue. The nationalist rejects the limitations on power and discretion which alliances with foreign powers, or participation in an international organization implies. The utopian internationalist rejects the partialism of security diplomacy and the sordidness of political and economic means. He worships in the pure church of humanity redeemed. In effect, but not in intent, he often finds himself lodged in the same isolationist pew with the nationalist.

The Foreign Policies of Veterans' Organizations

The veterans' organizations in the United States have historically placed special emphasis on a strong national defense policy. Their general ideology has been nationalist and patriotic, and they have led in efforts to suppress subversive elements. As an aspect of their nationalism they have shown strong distrust of foreigners, and they have advocated the restriction of immigration.

At the present time the larger veterans' organizations have become somewhat more internationalist in their foreign policy views, but their greatest concern still continues to be the strengthening of our military forces, the inculcation of patriotism and the suppression of subversive elements, and the maintenance of restrictions on immigration. It is of interest that the veterans' organizations of the older generation (the American Legion and the Veterans of Foreign Wars) are the more conservative and nationalist in their views, while the organizations restricted to veterans of World War II (AMVETS and the American Veterans Committee) tend to be more liberal and internationalist. This is particularly true of the American Veterans Committee.

The American Legion has been among the most active pressure groups which have urged the enactment of a universal military training law and a strong military establishment. At the same time, it has supported the European Recovery Program, Western union, and the North Atlantic Pact. It supports the United Nations and advocates the abolition of the veto in matters of aggression, also the strengthening of the International Court of Justice by giving it power to interpret aggression "with appropriate jurisdiction over individuals, corporations and nations in these matters." It also advocates the establishment of an effective world police force under direct control of the Security Council.[28]

The Veterans of Foreign Wars places an even stronger emphasis on unilateral national security measures. Thus it favored a modified version of the European Recovery Program to operate on a one-year basis after which its accomplishments would be reconsidered. Under no circumstances, its officers insisted, was such a program of foreign aid to interfere with a strong national security program for the nation.[29] "The enactment of universal military training and the retrievement of America's place as the No. 1 world air power are priority objectives of the VFW." [30] The organization was opposed to sharing atomic secrets with foreign nations, and advocated the return of atomic energy control to the military establishment.

The veterans' organizations of the younger generation have taken a broader view of domestic and foreign policy. The American Veterans Committee takes a moderate left position, while AMVETS represents itself as in the center of the political spectrum. One of the essential differences between the two younger-generation veterans' organizations has to do with their attitudes on national defense. AMVETS favors universal military training, selective service, the "largest air force in the world," a program of disaster instruction for civilians, and the prohibition of the shipment of war goods to Russia and her satellites. At the same time, AMVETS favors the European Recovery Program, the North Atlantic Pact and strengthening the United

Nations by eliminating the use of the veto. It has also come out in favor of a freer system of international trade and the formation of an international trade organization.[31]

The American Veterans Committee on the other hand has opposed universal military training and selective service. "We believe in the recruitment of such an armed force through voluntary enlistment and will support legislation to encourage such voluntary enlistment through the elimination of the caste system, increased pay, social security benefits, educational opportunities, and the removal of quotas based upon race, creed, or color." [32]

It condemned military aid to the "reactionary" regimes of Greece and China.[33] At a later time it approved the European Recovery Program, condemning "all efforts to amend this bill by cutting the total amount, by denying the four year commitment, by transferring control of the program from our representative government to a non-representative corporation and by requiring American political intervention in Europe through control of blocked European currencies, through opposition to nationalization, and through insistence on repayment by Europe in strategic materials or transference of bases." [34] In November, 1948, it took the further step of advocating the shipment of military supplies to Western Europe on a lend-lease basis, and the formation of a North Atlantic Pact.[35]

The American Veterans Committee is a strong supporter of the United Nations and has criticized all nations, including the United States, for violating the spirit of the Charter, and by-passing the various agencies of the international organization. It favors the calling of a world convention to amend the Charter of the United Nations to "enable it to enact, enforce, and interpret world law to prevent war." [36]

While the veterans' organizations have gone far in ranging themselves behind the various foreign aid programs, the United Nations, and the North Atlantic Pact, it is evident that the primary concern of the larger and older organizations is with American military power. There are strong nationalist overtones in many of their recommendations, and more of their energy and resources is devoted to these American security measures.

The Foreign Policies of Women's Organizations

The activities of American women's organizations in the field of national policy are co-ordinated through two top committees. The Women's Joint Congressional Committee serves as a clearing house for general matters in the field of national legislation. The Women's Action Committee for a Lasting Peace serves as a co-ordinating agency in the special field of foreign policy. Both of these over-all organizations and most of their constituent groups tend to be liberal in matters of social and economic policy, and internationalist in their foreign policy views. The effectiveness of these various women's organizations in their lobbying and propaganda activities is attested to in a periodical published by the National Industrial Conference Board.[37] The allegation made in this attack on the pressure activities of women's organizations is that a small group of "New Deal" and "pink" professional women lobbyists are improperly representing their views as those of American women in general. The evidence suggests that, on the whole, the women's organizations consult their membership more frequently and perhaps more effectively than most other types of pressure organizations. A second allegation is that these organizations present their memberships with "packaged thinking" and that there are no really effective processes of discussion through which policies are agreed upon. That this criticism is especially applicable to women's organizations is not supported by such evidence as is available.

Two points, however, may be made about the pressure group and opinion situation among women. First, women appear to be less well informed than men in the field of public policy, and considerably less definite in their views. We have already seen that the feminine sample in most public opinion surveys includes substantially more "don't know," "undecided," and "no opinion" responses. Secondly, the various opinion surveys show an "idealistic" and "internationalist" bias among women. Given these two conditions among American women, it is perhaps correct to conclude that the feminine activists in the various women's organizations have considerable discretion and influence in making organization policy. On the other hand, the liberal and internationalist trend in the policies of these organizations would appear to be representative of the stronger idealistic and humanitarian trend among the feminine component of the population.

Of the many women's organizations four have been selected for comment: the General Federation of Women's Clubs, the League of Women Voters, the National Federation of Business and Professional Women's Clubs, and the Women's Action Committee for a Lasting Peace. The General Federation of Women's Clubs is the largest and least specialized of women's organizations. It is most representative of the non-professional, middle- and upper-class housewife. It is perhaps the least critical among women's organizations of the various government publications and pamphlets which its Washington headquarters funnels into the thousands of constituent women's clubs throughout the country. The General Federation favored the renewal of the Reciprocal Trade Agreements Act "without crippling amendments," endorsed the International Trade Organization, and gave unqualified approval of the Marshall Plan. While it took no formal position on universal military training, it did support a temporary and limited selective service program. It favors the principle of World Federation and urged the government to initiate action to transform the United Nations into a "world law-making body with power to prevent war and to enforce justice upon individuals." [38] In its convention in April, 1949, the Federation approved the principle of the North Atlantic Treaty.[39]

The League of Women Voters, on the other hand, is representative of the more politically interested and active women in the United States. It is in a sense a "feminine civic elite." The rank and file of its constituent organizations plays an active role in policy-making which limits the scope of discretion of its Washington leadership. The League's record on foreign policy is not one of uncritical support of Administration proposals. Thus the organization was split on the question of Greek-Turkish aid. It took no position for or against the measure which was adopted, but urged that the program of aid be administered through the United Nations.[40] Its support of the Reciprocal Trade Agreements Act, the International Trade Organization, and the European Recovery Program was unqualified. While the League is strongly internationalist in its views, it has not taken an explicit position in favor of world government. It recommends serious study of such proposals and favors the continual expansion of the security powers of the United Nations. The League approved the North Atlantic Pact "without enthusiasm." A substantial portion of its membership opposed the Pact as undermining the spirit and powers of the United Nations. In order to meet this type of internal criticism it qualified its approval by asserting:

> "A universal system of collective security under the United Nations remains our goal. The pact should be used as a means toward that end, to give time in which a strong United Nations and stable peace can be built. This goal should be constantly kept to the fore. We urge our Government to continue to work toward reaching agreement in the United Nations on UN forces, the regulation of armaments, and the control of atomic energy." [41]

The National Federation of Business and Professional Women's Clubs is a conservative organization. It consists of a membership of more than a hundred thousand professional and business women organized in local groups which are federated in the national organization. It maintains close ties with the National Association of Manufacturers and the United States Chamber of Commerce. In contrast to the other women's organizations, it has taken a position in support of universal military training. Its support of the extension of the Reciprocal Trade Agreements Act was qualified by protectionist restrictions. It fully approved of the European Recovery Program. [42]

The Women's Action Committee for Lasting Peace was formed in 1943 for the purpose of mobilizing the efforts of women toward the formation of a collective security organization. It is both a constituent and an individual membership organization. Some fourteen national women's organizations, including the General Federation of Women's Clubs and the Y.W.C.A., are affiliated with the Women's Action Committee. Its field of interest is limited to foreign policy problems. For a large number of women's organizations—most of which do not have adequate personnel and facilities—it constitutes a specialized foreign policy lobbying and propaganda agency.[43]

The foreign policy views of the Women's Action Committee are quite similar to those of the League of Women Voters. It strongly favored the renewal of the Trade Agreements Act and the adoption of the European Recovery Program. Its position in the United Nations reflected a balancing of internationalist hopes against what they considered to be the real possibilities of the moment. It expressed skepticism as to the possibility of amending the United Nations charter to restrict the use of the veto, and consequently recommended that Article 51 be implemented "by a supplementary agreement, binding as many nations as may desire, in a pact of collective self-defense, as has already been done in the Western Hemisphere, and more recently in Brussels." [44]

In her testimony approving the North Atlantic Pact Mrs. Dana C. Backus, interim chairman of the Women's Action Committee, stated:

> "It may seem strange to some that an organization of women dedicated to the cause of lasting peace should be urging the ratification of a military pact, even though that pact is of a purely defensive nature. Because our hearts are set on lasting peace, it would be nice if we could join the ranks of those who feel that the way for this country to achieve peace is to say that we won't fight and that we will disarm. The difficulty with that isolationist-pacifist approach is that it won't work unless every nation agrees to it and puts it into practice. The other approach to lasting peace is through collective consultation to settle disputes and collective action to prevent or stop aggression." [45]

On the whole, the women's organizations are strongly internationalist in tendency, but their internationalism does not fit the stereotype of feminine idealism and naivete. All of the organizations discussed above approved the North Atlantic Pact, to be sure with qualifications and overtones of serious misgivings. Only one of these organizations—the General Federation of Women's Clubs—came out in favor of initiating steps toward the establishment of a world government. With the exception of the conservative National Federation of Business and Professional Women's Clubs, all of the women's groups favored the elimination of tariff barriers.

The Foreign Policy of Religious Organizations

The great majority of church organizations in the United States adhere to the foreign policy consensus. Thus the organizations representative of Protestant and Catholic opinion in the field of foreign policy—the Federal Council of Churches of Christ in America and the Catholic Association for International Peace—have consistently supported most of the foreign policy steps taken since the end of the war. However, the policies of both of these organizations are influenced by Christian pacifist attitudes which sometimes lead them to minimize military security considerations. But this is not to be confused with the type of religious pacifism discussed in the next chapter.

The Federal Council of Churches of Christ in America was organized as a general representative agency by twenty-five constituent Protestant denominations, claiming some twenty-seven million church members. The Council is controlled by a body of delegates named directly by the constituent denominations. An executive committee is empowered to make decisions in the interim between biennial sessions of the delegates.

The Council tends to be liberal in its domestic policy and internationalist in foreign policy. This has aroused some opposition among the more conservative and fundamentalist Protestant groupings. An organization called the American Council of Christian Churches has recently been formed which takes a more conservative and nationalist position on domestic and foreign policy. Nevertheless, its foreign policy position falls within the general framework of the foreign policy consensus.

The general spirit of the Federal Council's approach to foreign policy is reflected in its "Program for Peace" adopted at its 1948 meeting. "Our people should not rely on military strategy to meet Communist aggression. Such reliance is more apt to bring war than prevent it. There should be greater concentration on positive programs of an economic, social, political, and moral character." [46] However, such a position is not inconsistent with a program of armament and security diplomacy. It is a "pacifist, civilian" emphasis rather than genuine pacifism. The Federal Council is opposed to universal military training, but its constituent institutions are apparently not unanimous on this question.[47] When the Greek-Turkish aid issue arose the Council gave only qualified approval and urged that in so far as was possible the program should be administered through the United Nations.[48]

The Council is consistently in favor of the elimination of trade barriers, and has given full support to the expansion of the reciprocal trade program, and the formation of the International Trade Organization.[49]

There does not appear to be any significant difference of opinion on foreign policy questions as between the Protestant and Catholic organizations. Both groups have a "right, center, and left." There are, however, a number of organizational differences worth noting. Both Catholic and Protestant organizations constantly test their proposals for consistency with authoritative Christian ethical principles. But the Catholic groups, in addition, constantly relate their proposals to authoritative papal pronouncements. While there has been no occasion in the postwar period in which the Vatican has recommended policies in explicit conflict with those of the United States, it is not beyond the realm of possibility that such conflicts might arise in the future. In that event, and depending on the specificity and sanction of the Vatican position, the Catholic organizations may be confronted with problems of conscience which might result in a partial withdrawal from the foreign policy consensus. But at the present time even the issue of Franco Spain does not divide the population on religious lines. Although it is probably correct that such a policy is more of a Catholic than a Protestant preference, many Protestant Americans advocate the inclusion of Spain in the Western coalition on security grounds, and many Catholics oppose its inclusion on democratic grounds.

The Catholic Association for International Peace is an agency which operates under the aegis of the National Catholic Welfare Conference. This latter body is the general social policy organization of the Catholic Church. The Catholic peace group is not a general membership organization. It consists of a group of working committees which are designated by the national organization. In this sense, the policy recommendations of the Catholic Association for International Peace are not formally representative of Church opinion. They are policies which the committee members agree to advocate among their own local Catholic communities.

A distinctive note in the policy recommendations and discussions of the Catholic peace group is its practice of testing policies for their consistency with basic Catholic doctrine as expressed in the papal encyclicals. Thus, in its position on the Marshall Plan one of its supporting documents stated: "The members of the Catholic Association for International Peace have a responsibility to promote the Marshall Plan as it is the best method available at the present time for fostering peace, and as it is consistent with the peace objectives of Pope Pius XII." [50]

The Catholic group has taken a strong position in support of the United Nations and has joined those groups advocating limitations on the use of the veto in the Security Council. It also favors the expansion of the trade agreement program and the establishment of the International Trade Organization.[51] More recently the organization expressed approval of the North Atlantic Pact. "The North Atlantic regional pact for joint defense of the United States, Canada and Western Europe seems necessary. It is consistent with the U.N., and may fill gaps in the U.N. . . . This Committee urges its speedy ratification." [52]

Like the Protestant community, the Catholic population has an articulate nationalist and reactionary wing (just as it has a small pacifist and social revolutionary wing). Its reactionary tendencies are not organized at the present time on a national basis. It is a movement of a local character organized around local publications, leaders, and organizations.

The Foreign Policies of Ethnic Groups

The influence of foreign ethnic and linguistic groups on American foreign policy generally takes the form of efforts to enlist American support for policies affecting their homelands. Historically such influence was mainly directed toward traditional national aims such as the preservation or return of national territory, the achievement of national independence, or the protection of minority ethnic or religious groups in foreign countries from persecution by the dominant groups. At the present time these traditional ethnic pressures have to a considerable extent been assimilated into the struggle between East and West. Much of the foreign language group pressure emanates from minorities whose homelands have been incorporated into the Soviet orbit. By and large the most influential organizations and newspapers of the groups so affected are hostile to Soviet and Communist policy, and their efforts are directed at getting the United States to take up more actively the cause of regaining the independence of their home countries. Smaller but quite energetic foreign language groups and newspapers propagandize in favor of the "New Democratic" regimes in their home countries, and oppose American intervention in developments in those regions. In a logical sense these last groups belong in the following chapter in which Communist influenced groups are treated, but for purposes of unity they are included here.

According to the 1940 census, more than twenty million persons in the United States reported some language other than English as their mother tongue. In the same census some thirty-five million reported foreign birth, foreign parentage, or mixed parentage. This large sector of the population constitutes the audience for the more overt form of ethnic influence over foreign policy. It should not be forgotten that the older and dominant ethnic strata of the population—those from Northern and Western Europe—are certainly influenced in their foreign policy views by their ethnic backgrounds. Such influence, however, is reflected in less obvious and less organized ways. There is an unconscious community of interest between the older elements among the American population and the Western European culture area which tends to focus American attention in that direction and create sympathy for an active American foreign policy.

Loyalties to the foreign culture and the homeland are perpetuated through a variety of specialized institutions, media of communication, and organizations. There are almost a thousand foreign language publications in the United States published in some forty languages, with an estimated circulation of more than six million readers. In addition there are more than three hundred foreign language radio programs broadcast from about a hundred and fifty radio stations in twenty-seven different languages. Church congregations in which the services are in part conducted in the native languages of the parishioners have approximately fifteen million members. The membership in fraternal organizations and nationality associations among the foreign language groups is more than three million.[53]

The most significant and active foreign language organizations are those of the Jews, Germans, Italians, Poles, Irish, Czechoslovakians, Hungarians, Greeks, and Yugoslavs. In most cases the organizations representing these ethnic groups operate by themselves, but some of the Iron Curtain ethnic minorities have recently formed an over-all organization called the Federation of Americans of Central and Eastern

European Descent. They maintain headquarters in Washington and co-operate with the organization of refugee Eastern European political leaders often referred to as the "Peasant International." They advocate a liberal immigration program for displaced persons and a strong anti-Communist policy in the Eastern European area.

The Jews have been the most active single ethnic group in foreign policy questions in recent years. In this regard they have fallen heir to the role of the Irish-Americans in spreading anti-British sentiment and in advocating American intervention in British imperial questions.[54] This type of Irish influence has declined to a relatively minor pressure although vestiges still persist. Thus, the National Chairman of the Ancient Order of Hibernians, Michael A. McGrath, appeared before the Senate Foreign Relations Committee Hearings on the European Recovery Program to oppose aid to Britain unless the British permitted the unification of all of Ireland under the government of Eire.

> "The thousands of men and women enrolled in the membership of the Ancient Order of Hibernians and Ladies Auxiliary vigorously protest as American taxpayers the sending of one red cent to the British Empire for the purpose of maintaining a bridgehead in ancient Ireland, and to delay if possible the action of the large majority of the inhabitants of that ancient country to abolish the artificial boundary that has existed against all reason since 1920, and was set up by virtue of a shotgun treaty, reference to which has been made to your committee." [55]

The activity of Jewish organizations in the postwar period has been primarily directed at getting American support for the establishment of an independent Jewish nation in Palestine. A second aim has been the admission into the

United States of Jewish displaced persons. The largest Jewish organization in the United States is the Zionist Organization of America, claiming a quarter of a million members and with an annual budget of approximately $25,000,-000. Other organizations of a Zionist inclination are the Hadassah, a women's organization, a number of labor Zionist groupings, and the Revisionist groups which are sympathetic to the ultranationalist and "activist" political parties in Palestine. The membership claimed by all these groupings is just under seven hundred thousand. They are well financed, effectively organized, and have engaged in propaganda and lobbying activities on a large scale.[56] An over-all group called the American Zionist Emergency Council was recently formed to co-ordinate the activities of the individual Zionist groupings. This agency appeared before the resolutions committees of both major party conventions in the summer of 1948 to advocate unequivocal declarations of support of the new state of Israel.[57]

There is also an anti-Zionist movement among American Jews called the American Council for Judaism. This group is opposed to "Jewish nationalism," arguing that they are Jews in religion but not in nationality. It is supported by only a small element among the Jewish population but has been quite active in propaganda and lobbying activities.[58]

As in the case of Irish, German and Italian ethnic nationalism the ultimate pressure exercised by the Jewish minority is in the electoral process. This has been of special importance in the struggle for control of key states in which there are large Jewish populations, such as New York. Thus during a special congressional election to fill a vacancy in the Bronx, perhaps the main issue of the campaign was which of the two candidates—Leo Isaacson or Isidore Dollinger—took the stronger Zionist position.[59] Jewish pressure, during the electoral campaign of 1948 in favor of American support of the new state of Israel, influenced both parties to adopt "Zionist" planks in their party platforms.

Louis Bean, in his studies of election returns, provides some excellent evidence of the influence of ethnic groups in elections. He points out that in the 1940 election large pro-Willkie deviations from previous voting patterns were almost always associated with concentrations of German-Americans. This was true even in certain traditional Democratic counties in Texas where the German populations voted almost as a bloc for the Republican candidate. One outstanding exception to this pattern was Richmond County (Staten Island) in New York. Here, though the German population was small, there was a substantial loss of votes to the Democratic party. In this case it was a large Italian population reacting against President Roosevelt's "stab-in-the-back" speech which apparently accounted for the Republican gain.[60]

There are, of course, many other examples of "hyphenated-American" efforts to influence United States foreign policy. The struggle within various foreign language groups between those who oppose and those who favor Communist policy in the Soviet orbit is one of the most significant types of ethnic influence at the present time. The opponents of Communist domination often demand an extreme degree of intervention on the part of the United States. Thus the Co-ordinating Committee of American Polish Associations recently adopted a resolution calling for withdrawal of recognition of the governments of the Soviet orbit countries and the granting of recognition to the "governments-in-exile" in the United States. The trend of the speeches at this meeting was that it was not enough merely to prevent further Soviet aggression. Russia had to be driven back to her original borders. The Lithuanian-Americans currently insist that the United States induce Russia to withdraw her armed forces and Communist party apparatus from the territories of Lithuania, Latvia, and Esthonia. The Ukrainian-Americans go further back in history and insist on American aid for the re-establishment of the Ukrainian National Republic which was overrun by the Red Army in 1920.[61] Needless to say, the pressure of this type of ethnic nationalism among the Soviet orbit ethnic stocks, as well as the Zionists and other groups, often interferes with a balanced conception of American interests. Thus Zionist pressure has created problems in our relations with Great Britain and the Arab states of the Middle East. The understandable but extreme anti-Soviet feeling of Iron Curtain minorities in the United States may embarrass efforts at establishing economic relations with Eastern European countries on which the success of the European Recovery Program partly turns.

There can be little question that the great bulk of the foreign language groupings in the United States are anti-Communist. Nevertheless the Communist elites within these groupings are quite articulate and get a share of attention far out of proportion to their numerical support. Out of a total of almost eight hundred foreign language periodicals about thirty-five were found to be pro-Communist in a post-war study. The Communist publications have approximately five per cent of the total foreign language circulation in the United States.[62] On the whole, therefore, the foreign language groups in the United States may be included within the American foreign policy consensus. But the pro-Communist and extremely anti-Communist elements are deviational groupings. The pro-Communist groupings are included among those elements who reject the present American foreign policy and advocate appeasement of and concessions to the Soviet Union. The extreme anti-Communist groupings subordinate American interests to their conceptions of the interests of their homelands.

The groups described here are representative of the economic, religious, cultural, and ideological diversity of the United States. They are in agreement, with reservations of a more or less serious degree, with the development of American foreign policy since the end of the war. The overtly united American front in the field of foreign policy, however, is in large part a product of conditions which may change in the future. In the event of such change, what are at the moment mere reservations may turn into serious dissensions.

From this point of view, the most vulnerable element in our foreign program would seem to be our foreign trade policy. Perhaps it is only the gravity of the external threat to American interests which has made possible the continuance of the reciprocal trade program. Many business, labor, and farm organizations have accepted this policy with serious qualifications. Under less threatening circumstances the resistance to such a program of reducing American trade barriers may rise to a point at which further steps in the direction of freer trade become impossible.

This danger is especially serious in view of the attitudes of the public on the tariff issue. In the various surveys of this problem it appeared that only a minority of the respondents fully approved of a low tariff policy. If we add to those favoring such a policy the respondents who approved with qualifications we would find a bare majority who favor a freer foreign trade program. In one survey as many as 28 per cent of the respondents were undecided, while another 20 per cent opposed low tariffs. It is thus clear that the public is somewhat susceptible to protectionist arguments and that the present tariff policy lacks stable and widespread support.[63] It is not difficult to imagine circumstances in which powerful pressure groups could check the trend toward the elimination of trade barriers.

A second type of dissent within the foreign policy consensus arises out of a bias among significant elite groups and among large elements of the public against unilateral security measures. Only the gravity of the Communist threat has held these attitudes in check. This anti-security bias has both a pacifist and an internationalist element. The pacifist rejects measures of national defense and "security diplomacy"; the internationalist rejects partial security measures. A recent study of pressure group attitudes toward universal military training showed that some two hundred national and state organizations opposed training, while only seventeen groups supported it. Much of the opposition came from church and educational groups.[64] At the same time the public opinion polls have generally indicated widespread public support for military training (over sixty per cent). Nevertheless the articulate opposition to this program has been sufficient to prevent its enactment.

The "internationalist" dissent within the foreign policy consensus takes the form of an unwillingness to support partial security arrangements such as the North Atlantic Pact. At the present time none of the larger pressure organizations are opposed to the pact. However, this widespread public support[65] may persist only as long as the policy of the Soviet Union continues to be overtly aggressive. This is suggested by the strong overtones of reluctance which qualified the approval of many of the organizations which supported the treaty.

These weaknesses in public support for our present foreign policy are produced not only by such idealistic motivations as pacifism and internationalism, but also by a reluctance to accept the economic consequences of such an active program of security diplomacy. It is the rule in opinion surveys that the moment one suggests to respondents that their support for this or that means more taxes or costs for the United States there is some loss of enthusiasm and a shifting from support to opposition.[66] While this type of shifting in relation to the financial costs of Marshall Plan aid, and the arms program supporting the North Atlantic Pact, is not large, it suggests a public susceptibility to conservative economic arguments. It is quite possible that resistance to accepting the financial costs of the American security and world political position might substantially increase in the event of a serious domestic economic crisis or a temporary stabilization in foreign affairs. Even under present conditions policy-makers are generally confronted with considerable resistance on foreign policy measures specifically involving financial costs. The conservative political and pressure group elites resist adding charges to the national budget even though such an attitude is inconsistent with their foreign policy position.

Finally, the tendency of foreign language groups to set a high priority on the national interests of their home countries is a constant source of difficulty within the foreign policy consensus. It is not, and is not likely to become, as serious a problem as those described above. However, it may sometimes have the effect of involving us in the internal conflicts of foreign countries and areas in such a way as to result in a net diplomatic or security loss for the United States.

IX. Competing Foreign Policies

WHILE some of the organizations described in the preceding chapter deviated from the foreign policy consensus, the differences were comparatively slight in degree. The deviations described in the present chapter are substantial in nature in that they involve fundamental disagreement with regard to foreign policy values and procedures. The foreign policy consensus derives from an ideological consensus, a basic acceptance of the importance of reconciling individual freedom with mass welfare. The essential spirit of our foreign policy consensus derives from the will to maintain and foster this value compromise against the threat of Communist expansion. The Soviet and Communist elites are striving to suppress individual freedom in the interest of an alleged mass welfare, and of an alleged ultimate human emancipation.

The foreign policy consensus also involves an agreement on means. None of the groups so far described were fully inhibited in a normative sense from approving the use of any of the instrumentalities of foreign policy. They were capable of some degree of flexibility in considering the desirability of resorting to coercion or the threat of coercion implied in security diplomacy. Their general attitude toward means took into consideration the imperfections of man and his institutions; they did not count on any sudden moral or rational transformation of world politics which would resolve the age-old tension between "bad" means and "good" ends. Both with regard to means and ends the foreign policy consensus avoids absolutes and universals. The deviant groups, on the other hand, tend to seek absolutes and universals.

A typology of foreign policy deviations may bring a certain order to a situation which on the surface appears to be hopelessly complex. Such a classification proceeds from the basic definition of the foreign policy consensus. Those foreign policy proposals which differ in their approach to the basic ideology of American foreign policy may be described as "end" deviations. Here there are two main subtypes, the "radical appeasers" and the "reactionaries." The "radical appeasers" place extraordinary stress on the value of mass welfare and security and are less ready to defend the value of freedom. They are inclined to maximize the welfare and security achievements under Communism and minimize the terroristic and repressive features. Contrariwise, they are inclined to minimize the mass welfare achievements in the United States and maximize the repressive and discriminatory features of American social and political life. The "reactionaries" are at the other end of the foreign policy value spectrum. They place extraordinary stress on individual freedom as they define it and tend to oppose any measures of a welfare character which affect this narrowly defined conception of freedom. Thus the advocates of reactionary foreign policies tend to accept as allies those nations which oppose the invasion of the economic freedom in which they are particularly interested, even though its defense has resulted in the loss of political freedom (e.g., Spain), and tend to reject as allies nations in which economic freedom has been restricted in the interest of mass welfare (e.g., Great Britain). By virtue of this special approach to foreign policy values the "reactionary" finds it difficult if not impossible to accept the "Western coalition" now in the making and the basic value compromises on which it rests. He searches for a coalition in which his particular value emphasis is especially fostered, recommends measures that force particular nations to accept his value emphasis, or joins forces with the isolationists in rejecting any coalition.

The second major type of foreign policy deviation involves special approaches to the problem of political means. And here we may distinguish three subtypes—the pacifists, the nationalists, and the internationalists. The pacifist rejects force in principle, and a diplomacy based upon force. The nationalist tends to reject mutualism in diplomacy. He insists on unilateral measures as means to security. The internationalist, as the term is used here, tends to insist on universal and permanent measures of security and to reject approximations. These, of course, are pure types. The organizations whose policies are to be examined cannot be neatly catalogued. But the purpose of the classification will be served if it provides us with a set of polar types which define the dimensions of articulate opposition to our present foreign policy.

In the discussion of American character and foreign policy the hypothesis was advanced that American foreign policy moods swing back and forth between a set of poles. Idealism gives way to cynicism, optimism to pessimism, tolerance to intolerance, withdrawal reactions to interventionism. In the discussion of sociological groupings and the foreign policy mood the point was made that certain components of the population were especially susceptible to these moods.

While the moods of the general public fluctuate in response to changing experience, at the elite level there are persistent articulators of the various moods whose audiences increase and diminish in accordance with changes in the gen-

eral foreign policy mood. At one time the articulate nationalists or reactionaries are minor voices in the wilderness. At
another time their voices acquire a greater resonance, not
only among those social groupings which are especially susceptible to their views, but among the population as a whole.
From this point of view the foreign policy nationalists and
reactionaries are the persistent ideologues of pessimism,
cynicism, and intolerance. The pacifists and internationalists
are the permanent elites of idealism and optimism.

Radical Appeasement

This particular approach to foreign policy is primarily
characteristic of American Communists and "fellow travelers." Essentially, the radical appeasement position rests on a
strong dissatisfaction with economic, social, and political conditions in the United States, even though it operates from
the same fundamental value position as that of the consensus group. In principle, it accepts the twin ideals of welfare and freedom. But it systematically stresses the lack of
welfare and freedom in the United States. At the same time
the appeasers, while attaching validity to the value of freedom, definitely favor security and equalitarian values and
are ready to go some distance in qualifying freedom by
maximizing these other values. By such a value bias and
selection of data the radical appeasers are enabled to attack
the validity of a policy of firm resistance to Soviet-Communist expansion. They refuse to accept the American or Western resolution of the welfare-freedom problem as in any way
better than the resolution of this problem among the Communist countries. The American Communists view the Soviet
solution as immeasurably superior to that obtained in the
United States. The "fellow travelers" see the contrast in

more balanced terms. The Soviet Union is not morally better than the United States, but at the same time it is not significantly worse. The leading appeasement group in the United States at the present time is the Progressive Party, an organization which has absorbed or includes as constituent groups the Progressive Citizens of America, the American Labor Party, and the Wallace-for-President Committee. The Communist Party of America, the National Council of American-Soviet Friendship, the National Council of Arts and Sciences, and the Congress of American Women are a few of the other organizations which take this same foreign policy view.

With regard to the tendency of the appeasers to overstress evils in the United States and understress evil in the Soviet orbit a number of citations may be helpful. Thus Henry Wallace in his remarks on the North Atlantic Treaty before the Senate Committee evaded the question of civil liberties in the Soviet Union and pointed to the lack of civil liberty in the United States.

> *Senator McMahon:* When you disagree with the government in Russia, Mr. Wallace, you die; do you not?
>
> *Wallace:* I beg your pardon?
>
> *Senator McMahon:* You die, do you not, when you disagree with the government in Russia?
>
> *Wallace:* I do not know whether you die or not, but that is what the American press says.
>
> *Senator McMahon:* And the only reward that is preserved for you here is to weigh your ideas, and to accept them or reject them, as their worth is indicated to the people of the United States.
>
> *Wallace:* I certainly want to keep the United States that way, and I say there is grave danger that the United States will not be kept that way if we allow

ourselves to be overcome by this anti-Communist hysteria.[1]

In the field of foreign policy the Communists differ from their "front" organizations such as the Progressive Party. The Communists treat Soviet foreign policy as inherently peaceful and progressive, while that of the United States is inherently imperialistic and reactionary. The fellow-traveling Progressives treat Soviet foreign policy as an understandable response to Western provocation. Thus Senator Glen Taylor, in a speech to the Senate in opposition of the European Recovery Program, treated the Russian seizure of the border countries of Lithuania, Latvia, and Esthonia as an understandable reaction to Allied intervention after the first world war.

"Now, Mr. President, there has been a great deal of fuss because the Russians have reabsorbed the territories that were taken away from them. Might I ask this question: Suppose the Japs had whipped us in this recent war. Suppose they had taken Oregon, Washington, and California away from us and set them up as jumping off places in case they wanted to fight us again; that they had made each of those States an independent sovereign nation with a government acceptable to the Japanese. Mr. President, what do you think we would do under those circumstances the first time the opportunity presented? If I know the American people, I think we would take Washington, Oregon, and California back into the Union. But some people will say, 'The Lithuanians, the people of Latvia, and all those other hapless people did not want to be taken back by the Russians.' I wonder if California, Oregon, and Washington would want to come back into the United States after they had enjoyed sovereignty for 20 years or so. . . ."[2]

The appeasement groups have opposed every measure of resistance to Soviet expansion from the Truman Doctrine to the North Atlantic Pact. In place of these measures they have urged a policy of friendliness, withdrawal, and concessions, on the theory that these steps would allay Soviet anxieties about American aggressive intentions. It will be of interest to examine the evidence which is available as to the receptivity of the American public to this particular attitude toward the Soviet Union and to the policy of concessions advocated by these political groups.

In an intensive survey conducted by the Survey Research Center of the University of Michigan it was found that the great majority of respondents held the view that the Soviet Union had aggressive intentions.[3] Three out of four respondents felt that the Soviet Union had aggressive aims; two out of five stated that Russia wanted to rule the world. Only 3 per cent of the sample felt that Russia's aims were limited to the attainment of her own security. The survey also demonstrated that there has been increasing dissatisfaction with American policy toward Russia, and that most of this dissatisfaction was over an alleged lack of sufficient firmness on the part of the American government.

Thus only a very small percentage of Americans accept the radical appeasement view of Soviet aims. On the other hand, a much larger number are favorably disposed to a policy of continued negotiation with, and concessions to, the Soviet Union. Approximately two-thirds of the sample favored the continuance of negotiations, while approximately thirty-five per cent were ready to "give in to the Soviet Union on some points."[4] What form such concessions should take was apparently not clear in the minds of the respondents. They rather expressed general views that the United States should be flexible in its approach to Russia, and in the interests of peace should show a readiness to compromise. While this frame of mind suggests some susceptibility to appeasement arguments, it can hardly be equated with the specific "appeasement elite" position. Thus one respondent argued:

> "We could give in on some points, if we thought it would help to make a world peace. We can be wrong in some things as well as they can and anything is better than war unless we know it's wrong and unfair. On some points that don't matter we should be willing to give in but I'm afraid not on what they (Russia) want." [5]

What this "concessions mentality" appears to be is a frame of mind among a large sector of the population in favor of continued efforts to find an adjustment with the Soviet Union in view of the magnitude of the risks involved. Those who favor a program of concessions on the scale, and of the type, recommended by the appeasement elite appear to be extremely few in number, perhaps under five per cent.

As we have already seen in an earlier chapter the percentage of respondents taking relatively friendly views of Russian aims, and ready to make concessions to her, has decreased substantially since the end of the war. The decline in this favorable attitude has been in large measure a consequence of Soviet and Communist aggressions in the past four years. Thus opposition to appeasement seems to be associated with obvious aggressive actions on the part of the Soviet Union. For most Americans it would not appear to be based on an understanding of the nature of the Communist movement. Thus, only a third of a sample recognized the Communist movement as having aims of world expansion. A larger proportion tended to view the Soviet Union as being motivated by partial expansionist aims. This suggests a certain vulnerability toward overt changes in Soviet tactics. A temporary stabilization in Soviet foreign policy might strengthen the concessionist sentiment in the United States and undermine efforts at organizing an effective long-run security system.

Reactionary and Nationalist Foreign Policies

The advocates of reactionary foreign policies in most cases are nationalists as well. Since the essential spirit of reaction is intolerance of difference or change, those who are reactionary in matters of economic and social policy tend to be hostilely disposed toward relations of mutuality with foreign countries. This is subject to at least one outstanding exception. The reactionary and often the nationalist tend to be favorably disposed toward right-wing extremism in foreign countries. They have sympathy for authoritarian countries which have suppressed labor organizations and left-wing parties. This suggests the peculiar view of freedom which characterizes the ideology of reactionary movements in the United States. The essential freedom which the reactionary cherishes is the freedom of privilege. Political and social freedom have little meaning for him. He tends to be anti-democratic, anti-foreign, anti-Semitic.

A somewhat extreme example of a reactionary movement, and therefore particularly useful for analytical purposes, is the National Economic Council. This organization of some three thousand members is dominated very largely by a single individual, Merwin K. Hart. The spirit of this movement is reflected in an exchange of views between Hart and Senator Barkley during the hearings on the European Recovery Program.

Barkley: In your statement here you seem to condemn everything that has been done in this country in the last 15 years, and you even went back further than that by saying that even before that this Socialist virus had gotten into our blood. When did that start, in your opinion?

Hart: I think it started about the second decade of this century.

Barkley: How was it manifested, insofar as legislation is concerned?

Hart: As a matter of fact, I think the organization or outfit that did as much to promote socialism in this country as anything is the magazine "The New Republic" which was, I think, formed in 1916, which, though it never had a circulation of over 50 or 60 or 70 thousand, saw to it that that circulation went to opinion makers in the country, and that had a profound influence in laying the foundation for the New Deal and for what I call the departure from the American principles.

. . .

Barkley: Do you regard the Federal Reserve System as an evidence of a socialistic trend in this country?

Hart: I think it was in a way, yes, Senator. . . .

Barkley: Do you regard the legislation which we have passed here a good many years ago known as the National Labor Relations Act, and the Wages and Hours Act, as Socialist?

Hart: I think that was one of the most vicious acts ever passed by the Congress.

Barkley: And it complies with your definition of socialism?

Hart: It certainly would tend very strongly in that direction. I think the fact that this Congress substantially amended it would tend to indicate that the Congress did not like it.

. . .

Barkley: Do you think the Social Security System, set up by Congress, providing for employment insurance is Socialist?

Hart: I think it is unsound for the Federal Government to be doing that, yes.

Barkley: It is Socialistic, according to your definition?

Hart: I think it is.[6]

On another occasion the Hart organization went even further in its development of this extreme anti-welfare position. One of its spokesmen argued,

"It was when the United States Supreme Court declared the social security law constitutional on May 24, 1937, that I first became convinced that the American way of life was ended beyond resuscitation in our day and generation. . . .

"Every item of this program [social security]—and to go farther back into its beginnings, occupational disease insurance, workingmen's compensation, the graduated income tax, the inheritance tax and compulsory State schooling—was an integral part of the Marxian plan, specifically and admittedly designed for the destruction of the capitalistic system. . . ."[7]

The extraordinary stress placed by reactionaries on the elimination and avoidance of governmental restraint is reflected in the position taken by the National Economic Council on military conscription and expenditures for national defense. The Council's argument urged that the main problem before the United States was the elimination of Communists and collectivists from high places in the American bureaucracy.

". . . if the Congress passes regimenting measures such as these, without first cleaning out from the government those persons, many of them Communist or communistic, responsible for these destructive policies—if, indeed, it does not take immediate steps to remove every Communist or fellow traveler from any public office he holds—then the passage of this regimenting legislation would be largely fruitless because the American people would continue to be betrayed in the future." [8]

Expenditures for military purposes are attacked by the National Economic Council since they undermine the free-enterprise system by requiring heavy taxation. The central principle in the ideology of the Council is the return to American economic and political orthodoxy. This social and political system which is alleged to have obtained in the period before the first world war is set forth as a kind of utopia. If we return to this ideology then all of our problems, domestic and foreign, will disappear.

Starting from this orientation the Council has opposed most American foreign policy measures since the end of the war. One exception has been the program of Greek-Turkish aid. It justified intervention of this kind, just as it favors recognition of Spain and the granting of aid to that country because of its "healthy" anti-Communist policies. In this regard the Council is consistent with its earlier policies toward Nazi Germany and Fascist Italy. While it did not give wholehearted approval to the policies followed by the fascist countries, it strongly approved their anti-Communism and opposed American participation in World War II.

The Council opposed the Marshall Plan as a scheme to "finance socialism in Europe." It favored a limited program of consumer goods relief frankly used to "convert Europe back to private enterprise." [9] The United Nations and its affiliated organizations is attacked as an octopus leading to a "statist, collectivist world."

> "The method of putting this deception over on the American people is simple. While we are lulled into imagining that the UN is all mouth, a harmless debating society, the Planners are busy attaching tentacles to its body—tentacles specially designed to grip hard just where they are intended to grip. These tentacles are 'agencies' of the UN. We are counted upon to assume naively that the agencies of a harmless body must be harmless too." [10]

The views of the Council on the North Atlantic Treaty represent as systematic a statement of the reactionary-nationalist position as can be found. The pact is bitterly rejected as an abandonment of the historic American policy against permanent alliances. It is described as a sure course toward "war and ruin"—through military overcommitments and financial bankruptcy. In place of the Treaty the Council proposes the following program: American freedom of action should be preserved by the avoidance of permanent commitments; every Communist and Communist sympathizer should be rooted out of the government and its agencies; our own decks should be cleared for action "by reducing our government expense and rejecting the whole Truman program for a socialized welfare state." Finally, it favors the establishment of a "real Western Hemisphere defense zone." "The Iberian Peninsula is probably the only area in the Continent capable of sustained defense. A Western Hemisphere defense zone can be created without the alliances, without bankruptcy or socialization of our own economy. Such defense is within our means." [11]

Similar in its views to the National Economic Council is the American Coalition of Patriotic Societies—a merger of some eighty-five organizations. Among its constituent members are branches of the Daughters of the American Revolution, the American War Mothers, the Dames of the Loyal Legion of the United States, the Military Order of the Loyal Legion, the Sons of the American Revolution, the Order of Colonial Lords of Manors in America, and similar groups. The Coalition formulates its policies at periodic conventions. The leader of the organization, John B. Trevor, described the policy-making process in the following terms.

> *Trevor:* What we do is this: The representatives of the societies meet in convention, and then the resolutions are printed and forwarded to the societies for their individual approval. Sometimes we get approval, sometimes they make no comment at all, and we take it that if they do not object to any of these resolutions it may be assumed fairly that that is the viewpoint of their organization. I should point out, possibly, that the president of each society is a member of the board of directors, and one other delegate elected or selected as the society may determine is the other delegate to the convention.
>
> *Chairman:* How many of these presidents of the 85 societies were present when these resolutions were adopted?
>
> *Trevor:* I think 35, sir—35 representatives directly were present at this meeting, but there were many members of these other societies present. The total attendance was 172.[12]

In its Resolutions of 1949 the American Coalition described the "National Socialist Planners," not the Communists, as the real enemy of the American system.

> "By disclaiming all connection with Communism, our National Socialist Planners in the government, in the labor unions, in the press and colleges and in our po-

litical parties have succeeded in relieving themselves of suspicion of subversive activity. But it is they who are our real enemies. It is they, rather than the Communists, who are doing the real job of destruction upon our society. It is they whom we must identify and defeat and remove from every post of authority and influence from which they make war upon our culture, our laws, our traditions and our freedom." [13]

The Coalition has taken a position in opposition to the United Nations, the International Trade Organization, and the Reciprocal Trade Agreements program. It also recommends the immediate cessation of all immigration into the United States. It has bitterly opposed the Marshall Plan and the North Atlantic Treaty. Like the National Economic Council, it demands the recognition of the Franco regime in Spain and its inclusion in the American program of aid. It opposes the North Atlantic Treaty "because there are implications throughout the North Atlantic Treaty that the State Department may have in mind such a co-ordination of our American economy with the economy of the signatory powers, and ultimately, perhaps, of the world as to constitute a major threat to the standard of living and safety of the people of the United States." [14]

The Economic Council and the American Coalition differ in foreign policy questions in only one essential; the first organization opposes universal military training, the second supports it. This illustrates a difference of approach within the body of reactionary-nationalist sentiment. The Economic Council is reactionary and nationalist in its ideology but also tends to be isolationist. It argues that if we return to a policy of economic and political orthodoxy there will be no need for regimentation of manpower and excessive expenditures for military purposes. If we just cut out the sin that is among us, we will be militarily and politically unassailable. If we fail to pluck out the evil, no amount of militarization will help us. The Coalition, on the other hand, is ready to accept the military and economic consequences of the nationalist position. They are ready to accept military conscription and expenditures for armaments.

The reactionary-nationalist position represents both an ideological and a means deviation from the foreign policy consensus. It rejects mass welfare as a fundamental policy aim. The only kind of desirable mass welfare is that which is achieved through a system of economic freedom from governmental intervention. It also rejects mutuality in diplomacy and urges that we would be safer if we were to "go it alone," or at best, in alliance with safely anti-Communist countries even when such countries are authoritarian.

The membership of these organizations is not significantly large. However, this point of view has a significant hold within the communications elites. The Hearst and McCormick press, for example, have enormous circulations. But reactionary nationalism, like radical appeasement, is of significance not because it commands a large and fully indoctrinated audience, but because some of its ideas reflect more widespread attitudes of suspicion, distrust, and withdrawal among the American population. Some impression of the extent of this potential audience may be gained from the survey materials on foreign policy attitudes.

Thus, while the great majority of respondents in surveys favor the Marshall Plan, a substantial minority (16 per cent) as recently as November, 1948, opposed its renewal.[15] Twenty-two per cent refused to venture an opinion. The proportion of respondents which has supported the North Atlantic Pact has ranged from two-thirds to three-fourths ever since the Treaty has been up for public discussion. Between fifteen and twenty per cent have opposed the negotiation and ratification of the Pact.[16] On the question of the inclusion of Spain among the Pact countries—a policy advocated by the reactionary-nationalist organizations—23 per cent favored its inclusion, 23 per cent were opposed, and 12 per cent had no opinion. Forty-two per cent were not familiar with the Franco regime and were not included in the figures given above. While there were some differences between Catholic and Protestant respondents they were not so large as might have been expected. Thus 25 per cent of the Protestants polled were opposed to the inclusion of the Franco regime as compared with 18 per cent among the Catholics.[17]

On the question of the general persistence of nationalist-isolationist sentiment a number of surveys show that perhaps more than a fourth of the population is susceptible to this type of appeal. The Survey Research Center of the University of Michigan on four separate occasions asked a sample of respondents: "Some people think that since the war this country has gone too far in concerning itself with problems in other parts of the world. How do you feel about this?" In December, 1946, 32 per cent agreed or agreed with qualifications. In October, 1948, the same result was reported. In January, 1948, 23 per cent felt that the United States had become too involved in foreign intervention.[18]

It is of interest that more respondents give an isolationist response when confronted with a general question than when confronted with a specific issue. It would therefore appear that some of this isolationism is a matter of feeling or mood which is not pressed when it comes to a question of specific policies. It may also be argued that even among those who accept the current trend of foreign policy there is a strong nostalgia for an earlier era of world politics which did not make such strident and persistent demands on our attention, or intellectual capacity and resources. The explicit isolationism of the reactionary-nationalist ideologues finds a slight echo in most of us.

Thus one might say that the foreign policy consensus is flanked on the "right" side by ideological fundamentalism and xenophobia, just as it is flanked on the "left" by ideological radicalism and internationalism. The reactionary elites play on the moods of a much larger audience which has accepted our foreign policy involvements with serious misgivings. These misgivings have been somewhat quieted by the obvious threat of Soviet-Communist expansion. It is important to remember that the suppression of these doubts and misgivings is tied up with an obvious threat. Should the threat appear to subside, these feelings of distrust of foreign countries and ideologies may have an opportunity for more unequivocal expression.

Pacifist Foreign Policies

There are many types and shadings of pacifism.[19] If we examine these groups from the point of view of the authority from which they derive their position we may distinguish between religious and secular pacifism. If we view them from the point of view of their readiness to accept international involvement we may distinguish between isolationist and internationalist pacifism. But all pacifist groups have in common a rejection of force in foreign affairs and the elaboration of some system of beliefs which renders force, preparation for force, and a diplomacy based upon force not only immoral, but also unnecessary. Perhaps it might better be put as follows: to the pacifist, force cannot be necessary *because* it is immoral. The pacifist operates with a voluntaristic conception of good and evil and a faith in the exemplary effects of good action. If one of the parties to a controversy can be made to act according to good precepts, then his opponent is bound to follow suit. Thus the pacifist is constantly driven in the direction of moral flagellantism. He is a follower of the injunction in St. Matthew, "Why beholdest thou the mote that is in thy brother's eye, but considerest not the beam that is in thine own eye?" He makes no objective measurements of the comparative size of optical obstructions, but in principle magnifies his own moral shortcomings. In such a pacifist as Milton Mayer this reaches the proportions of Gothic suffering and compassion.

> "I cry peace, peace and there is no peace. I speak with the tongues of men and of angels, and there is no peace. I have the gift of prophecy, and understand all mysteries and all knowledge, and there is no peace. I feed the poor and give my body to be burned, and there is no peace. Since I believe that what the Lord said is true and righteous altogether, I am compelled to believe that the reason there is no peace is that I have not enough faith, hope, and love to be very much of a pacifist." [20]

The philanthropic and humanitarian activities of the Society of Friends in foreign countries has gained for it a world-wide respect. It was the first in the field after both world wars to undertake humanitarian and "reorientation" programs in the defeated countries. In activities such as these, the Quakers have proceeded on the basis of rational as well as ethical calculation, and have achieved impressive results. The foreign policy position of the Quakers, however, is based on their traditional Christian pacifism.

The Society of Friends exercises its general foreign policy influence through the Friends Committee on National Legislation, a representative body meeting once or twice a year. The General Committee elects an Executive Committee which is empowered to act in the interval between general meetings.

The Friends Committee has accepted that part of American foreign policy which is not based on military or diplomatic security considerations. Thus they have approved the Reciprocal Trade Program, and American participation in the United Nations. They favor the strengthening of the United Nations and its ultimate establishment as a World Government. On the other hand, they reject selective service and universal military training, the American program of rearmament, and the North Atlantic Pact. In the case of the European Recovery Program they approved aid to Europe, but recommended that it should be made available to all countries, that it should not be directed against any country or countries, and that its administration should be turned over to the United Nations at the earliest moment.

The Friends Committee does not whitewash Soviet and Communist actions. It agrees that Marxism "stands in the way of an acceptance of the idea of peaceful coexistence." But it argues that Communism is sufficiently flexible to change if "new historical conditions" made it appear advantageous to do so. The United States could establish such conditions if it were to include the Soviet orbit in its program of aid, abolish the Western German state in favor of a unified and neutralized Germany, take a more conciliatory approach toward the Soviet Union, and continue efforts at disarmament.[21]

This group has conveniently restated its foreign policy position in justifying its opposition to the North Atlantic Pact.

"We oppose (1) attempts to form a North Atlantic Security Pact and other proposals for armed alliances in the guise of regional arrangements under the United Nations, because these, we believe, will further solidify the existing divisions in the world instead of reducing these divisions and fostering the unity necessary for peaceful cooperation; (2) establishment of bases in, or a military alliance with, Spain; (3) efforts to mis-direct the Benelux agreements into a military alliance; (4) the building of military bases in former mandated and colonial areas; (5) the policy of attempting the containment of Russia by military pressure, because it bypasses the United Nations and retards the development of security through truly international action." [22]

Quite similar in its foreign policy views to the Friends is the pacifist sect, the Church of the Brethren. This confession, operating through the Brethren Service Commission, occasionally sends representatives to Congressional Committees. In its critical statement on the North Atlantic Treaty its spokesman argued:

"The spread of certain ideologies across the world is greatly feared by many people of this country. Our commission believes that the best and the only ultimately successful method to stop this spread is through satisfying fully the basic physical, economic, personality, and spiritual needs of war-devastated and other underprivileged peoples. We believe the North Atlantic Treaty not only fails to give these basic satisfactions but also tends to hamper and retard present efforts in the direction of reconstruction." [23]

Even more representative of integral pacifism is the Fellowship of Reconciliation. This interdenominational organization places an extraordinary emphasis on individual conscience to the point of developing a martyrology of persons who have accepted the consequences of their opposition to war. These include conscientious objectors, persons refusing to register for the draft, and persons refusing to pay taxes because the proceeds are used for military purposes. Other pacifist organizations do not go quite so far in urging resistance to the authority of the state.[24] The testimony of a representative of the Fellowship on the North Atlantic Treaty illustrates the integral pacifists' complete faith in love and brotherhood. The Friends are far more circumspect and analytical in their policy recommendations. They develop a reasoned argument. The Fellowship of Reconciliation leans more in the direction of the apocalyptic and the prophetic mode of discourse.

"There are two Americas known throughout the world, as anyone who travels in Europe or Asia will testify. One is the America which is conscious of its power and conceited over its prestige and determined to use any means, however ruthless, to have its way. The Atlantic Pact is part of the program of such an America, vigorous, aggressive and unyielding. The other America, known and loved throughout the world is the generous America pouring out its bounty to those in any form of need in Europe or Asia, asking no return or reward for the sharing of the blessings which God has bestowed upon our Nation's life.

"We cannot permanently be both kinds of a country. We cannot lead both by force and by friendship. The issue which this pact presents to us will to a considerable degree determine the kind of America the world will know for decades, and perhaps for centuries, to come.

"We can be proud of our economic and military power, but that price will come at the cost of the affection of the peoples of the world. Or we can try to find our pride and power, which lies in the spiritual leadership. We can propose and sponsor movements for steady disarmament among the nations of Eastern Europe as a man talks with a man, yielding no sacred convictions of our own but recognizing that the most sacred conviction which men can have is human brotherhood." [25]

The secular pacifist operates with a system of humane rather than divine ethics. While it is not inherent in the secular pacifist position to be less complete in its rejection of violence than religious pacifism, in actual practice the secular movements tend to take a more equivocal position on the ethical nature of violence in international affairs. The non-denominational pacifist organizations include believers and non-believers. On the whole the religious components of these organizations tend to be more moderate in their views than the members of the pacifist religious sects.

The American Socialists of the Norman Thomas persuasion, operating through the Socialist Party, constitute one of the largest and most influential secular pacifist groups. Similar in conviction to the Socialist Party is the Post War World Council, a non-political membership organization. Another group is the National Farmers Union which, while a general agricultural pressure group, in its foreign policy position falls into the pacifist internationalist classification.

The Socialist Party and the Post War World Council are more explicitly opposed to Communism than are the religious pacifist groups. However, this opposition does not lead them to favor a strong security system to oppose Communist expansion. The Council tirelessly urges the United States to propose a program of universal disarmament. If the Soviet leadership refused to accept disarmament, then the United States should appeal to the masses of the Soviet Union and Eastern Europe. Thus Norman Thomas stated:

"Should America, strongest of nations, propose this disarmament, it would answer as nothing else can, charges of militarism and imperialism against us. Of course, there must be effective international control and that means reforms in the Security Council, and an international security force, probably a quota system. Should the Kremlin at first refuse these controls, nations outside the Soviet bloc, on a clearer issue than now exists, might pool their spiritual and material resources for security. Mr. Bevin's Western European alliance, or any enlargement of it, would have a far better basis should it follow this appeal for disarmament. I crave for my country the glory of initiating it." [26]

This argument of Norman Thomas does not preclude the possibility of a security policy. It urges that measures of this type be postponed as a last resort until all other avenues have been thoroughly explored. This theme of universal disarmament is the main argument advanced by the Socialist Party and Post War World Council in the place of our present foreign policy. It has been offered in the place of the draft and universal military training, military aid to Greece and Turkey, and the North Atlantic Pact. On the other hand, these groups favor the European Recovery Program and the various measures proposed to reduce trade and tariff barriers. The followers of Norman Thomas also advocate the ultimate development of the United Nations into a "truly democratic federal world government." [27]

The Farmers Union takes a position quite similar to that of the Socialists. Like the Socialists it opposed our entrance into World War II. Since the end of the war it has opposed military conscription, expenditures for armaments, the Greek-Turkish aid program, and the North Atlantic Pact. At the same time it has favored the elimination of trade barriers, and the formation of a world government on the foundation of the United Nations.[28]

While favoring the principle of the Marshall Plan the Farmers Union has urged that the program be carried out through the agencies of the United Nations. The reasoning of the Farmers Union leadership on the question of international security was interestingly reflected in the testimony of its legislative representative on the Greek-Turkish aid bill. After arguing that the most effective way of combating Communism was by "affording the masses of the Greek people the means for building a permanently productive economy," Russell Smith states:

> "We should like to emphasize to this committee the further danger that a venal government, once its army has been rebuilt and made powerful with American funds, may very easily change allegiance. In the European game of power politics such about faces have by no means been infrequent. Thus it may very well turn out if we pursue the course laid out here, that we have only spent our money to strengthen a potential enemy. If we must pour additional millions of tax money down the drain of military expenditures then let us at least strengthen our own military forces rather than those of foreign powers." [29]

These remarks illustrate the ambivalence of this type of pacifism on the score of international involvement. The Socialists and radical agrarians are ready to go the limit of internationalism as long as the means are unequivocally moral. Thus they favor free trade, world government, and the export of American resources to improve standards of living abroad. But security diplomacy and the threat of military sanctions tend to be rejected. If internationalism involves such moral and expedential risks, then better to withdraw entirely from such sordid machinations.

Thus there is in pacifist internationalism, religious and secular, an isolationist consequence if not an isolationist intent.[30] They start from the premise that the world is capable of moral regeneration through unequivocally moral means. If the world should turn out to be so morally complex as not to yield to this simple ethical rationalism, then they are ready to withdraw from it until it is prepared to receive their moral mission.

There is little in the public opinion surveys to suggest the degree of public receptivity to the appeals of the pacifist elites. Opposition to the various measures of national defense and security rests on many grounds. Only a small part of such opposition is based on pacifist premises. What evidence there is suggests that the pacifists have an extremely small audience of convinced believers. On the other hand, many of the larger and more influential organizations have a pacifist bias in that they accept national defense and security measures with considerable reluctance. This type of inhibition against security-oriented thinking represents a more serious problem in policy-making than the absolutism of genuine pacifism.

Internationalist Foreign Policies

If the pacifists tell us that war cannot be necessary because it is immoral, the extreme internationalists tell us that world government is possible because it is necessary. Both positions at the extreme rule out moral approximations and compromises. They are value absolutists. The extreme internationalists rule out the nation state and the security diplomacy system of the nation states. Out of that system of means, they believe, only evil can come; out of world government only good can come.

Actually the proponents of the pure faith of world government have been decreasing in numbers. Only one of the various groupings may be described as an absolutist "world government now" organization. This is the committee under the chairmanship of Chancellor Robert M. Hutchins of the University of Chicago. The committee itself was formed in 1945 shortly after the dropping of the atomic bomb on Hiroshima; it set itself the specific task of drafting a constitution for a world state.[31]

Its draft constitution was made public in March, 1948. Four principles were advanced to justify the constitution and the proposal for the immediate convening of a world convention. These were:

1. War must and can be outlawed. Peace must be universally enacted and enforced.
2. World government is the only answer to world destruction.
3. World government is necessary, therefore it is possible.
4. The price of world government and peace is justice.[32]

The constitutional system proposed is based on American federal principles. The federal government would have enumerated powers, mainly limited to keeping the peace and the joint development of global resources. Federal power would be binding on the individual. A federal supreme court would police the boundaries between state and central authority. A Federal Convention with one delegate for each million of population would serve as an electoral body to choose the president, the legislative council, and a "Tribune of the People." [33]

In defending the constitution Hutchins stated: "If it [World Government] fails because Russia refuses to join a just world government, then world government can do the next best thing to averting war. It can make the establishment and survival of a just world government the purpose of the war. A war fought on that issue would be the first in human history to be a war for the sake of peace." [34] The Hutchins group rules out such proposals as the North Atlantic Union,[35] or any other approximations of unification.

The largest organization among the advocates of world government is the United World Federalists, a consolidation of world government organizations established in February, 1947. It has almost five hundred chapters and is especially strong among college students. Its techniques include mass petition campaigns, meetings and revivals, special work with church and student groups, as well as aggressive lobbying at both the state and national level. The Federalists propose to bring pressure to bear on national policymakers by means of an enormous grass roots campaign. They have had world government resolutions introduced in all forty-eight state legislatures.

Whereas they originally took a world government approach to all questions of foreign policy, more recently they have reacted to specific foreign policy proposals. They have become more gradualist in their views and have been willing to recognize some foreign policy measures as approximations of their aims.

The aims of the group are to transform the United Nations into a world government by giving it a limited but genuine jurisdiction. The United Nations must have power to prohibit the manufacture or ownership of the means of organized warfare. It must have the power to prohibit the use of force in the settlement of international disputes. A world judiciary must have the power to try violators of the basic security law. An international inspectorate must have free access to all countries to investigate violations of the security law. A world police force, subject only to United Nations jurisdiction, must have a monopoly of modern weapons.

The structure of the United Nations is to be modified, with the present Assembly becoming a legislative body and the Security Council an executive cabinet.[36]

These changes are to be achieved within the framework of the United Nations. Under Article 109 of the present Charter a general conference of United Nations members is to be called. This conference is to become the constitutional convention. Amendments to the Charter require the approval of two-thirds of the nations represented and ratification by two-thirds of the nations, including all the permanent members of the Security Council. Recognizing that the Soviet Union would probably veto the revision of the Charter, the United World Federalists propose that the Charter be disregarded in this ratification requirement. Like the framers of the American Constitution the Convention could agree on a less than unanimity requirement among the Security Council members.

> "The delegates would be just as bold and just as wise [as the Philadelphia Convention] if they ignored the Charter of the United Nations and provided in the new instrument for its own ratification on more moderate terms. If two-thirds of the nations can write a constitution it would seem reasonable that two-thirds of the nations could establish it among themselves. Once this federation is established among a reasonable proportion of the world's nations, it forms an open and easily expansionable system. For any nation that did

not want to come in at first, there would always be a vacant chair." [37]

The United World Federalists do not oppose the North Atlantic Pact. They view it as a simple expedient "without doubt essential to our defense." They refer to one hazard in relation to the treaty, that expedients will be confused with ultimate objectives, "that emergency measures necessary in a time of crisis will be mistaken for long-range policy goals." A representative of the organization asked the Senate Foreign Relations Committee to make it clear that the Pact was an emergency measure and that the

". . . long range objectives of the United States are to so develop and greatly strengthen the institutions of the United Nations that in all good common sense we can depend on the United Nations for that security which we now seek through competitive armaments, alliances and other measures of power politics.

"Therefore I urge that we recognize the necessity of attempting, simultaneously with the implementation of the Pact, a realistic, general settlement of outstanding issues with the Russians and the simultaneous amendment of the United Nations Charter so as to transform the United Nations into a limited World Government. Neither of these processes should involve a policy of appeasement." [38]

There has undoubtedly been a development in the direction of political realism among the world government advocates. Most of them now appear to recognize that until the world institution is established, short-run diplomatic and security "expedients" are essential. But even their present degree of realism fails to recognize the enormous difficulties and dangers involved in the establishment of such a governmental system. They do not exclude national security diplomacy as completely sinful and futile, as does the Hutchins group. Their lack of realism arises from their strong need to simplify both problems and solutions.

Among the smaller international government groups and committees are Ely Culbertson's Citizen's Committee for United Nations Reform, and the Clarence Streit-Owen Roberts "Union of the Free" movement. The approach of the Culbertson group is to approximate the ultimate end of world federation by means of immediate changes in the Charter of the United Nations. The Culbertson "ABC" program involves (1) the abolition of the Security Council Veto in matters of aggression, (2) the control of atomic energy and other important weapons, and (3) the establishment of an effective but tyranny-proof world police force. The quota-force plan involves an active contingent at the disposal of the Security Council recruited from the small nations only, and five national contingents from the major powers held in reserve. Culbertson claims for his proposal that by means of three simple amendments, the ABC plan will transform the United Nations into a federal structure.[39]

The approach of the Culbertson group differs from that of the world federalists proper in a number of respects. The world federalists are ready to entrust an arms monopoly to a world government. The Culbertson committee opposes this on grounds that it might lead to world tyranny. It provides that individual nations may retain their own forces. There is some disagreement as to the jurisdiction of the world government over nations and individuals. Finally, both groups provide that the organization should go ahead in the event of a Russian refusal to join, leaving the door open for a future Russian change of heart.

The Streit-Roberts movement is organized at the present time in the Atlantic Union Committee for a Federal Convention. Its honorary president is former Supreme Court Justice Owen J. Roberts; its vice-presidents are former Undersecretary of War Robert Patterson and former Undersecretary of State Will Clayton.

The proposal of this group represents a post-North Atlantic Pact adaptation of an earlier proposal by Clarence Streit for a "Union of the Free." Streit has been urging the calling of a federal convention of the "nations most experienced in governing themselves on a basis of equal individual freedom." Such a convention should consider the formation of a federal union "in which the citizens are equally sovereign and divide the powers of government between the representatives they elect to their federal and their national government. A federal government is also so constituted in its legislative, executive, and judicial organs as to safeguard equally the more populous and less populous nations in it against domination. A federal government is also so constituted as to resemble the national governments in being directly responsible to the people, and in operating directly on the citizens through its own law-enforcing agencies in the few fields where they give it jurisdiction." [40] In the spring of 1949 the Streit and Roberts groups joined forces in efforts to turn the Atlantic Pact countries into an Atlantic Union of the Free. It was argued that such a federal union would provide a much stronger deterrent to Communist aggression than the present pact, that it would give the political and psychological initiative to the Western democracies, and that it would result in a much more efficient utilization of economic and military resources.[41]

The Atlantic Union group appears to be quite close in its position to the present foreign policy consensus. It might be described as falling within the consensus, but striving to draw it in the direction of greater internationalism. This

organization as well as the more ambitious world government groups have strong support in the Congress, among the
pressure groups, and in the public itself. Thus, during 1946
and 1947, in three separate surveys the American Institute
of Public Opinion found more than fifty per cent of its
respondents in favor of "strengthening the UN to make
it a world government with power to control the armed
forces of all nations, including the U.S." [42]

In another series of surveys the *Fortune* poll found a
quite substantial approval for the idea of world government.
Thus in December, 1948, around a third of its respondents
favored "taking steps right away to form a world government." Another third favored going ahead in this direction but more slowly. There would appear to be little question that the public mood is receptive to such proposals as
were discussed above. Whether they would be ready to
accept the political and financial consequences of such moves
it is impossible to say. Certainly doubts would increase as
the complex problems of representation and taxation became
matters of formal decision.

This analysis of competing or alternative foreign policies
has in effect provided us with a typology of American isolationism. Each one of the movements described constitutes
a special type of isolationism. Thus, the Communist elements among the appeasement groups are isolationist because they consider it to be desirable that the Soviet Union
should hold the initiative in world politics. The non-Communist Wallaceites are isolationists because they have a deep
distrust of the political motives and consequences of the
American initiative in world politics. The reactionary-
nationalists are isolationist because they distrust foreign
peoples and ideologies and have little confidence in the

soundness of the present political leadership in the United States. The pacifists (even those who advocate the most utopian internationalism) are isolationists because they reject the most essential means of politics, and deny us the right to be effective in the international sphere in defending our values. Finally, the extreme internationalists are isolationists because they reject those measures of partial international security which are possible today, and hold out but the one hope of universal salvation. "Not every one that saith unto me, Lord, Lord, shall enter into the kingdom of heaven."

Of all the deviational foreign policy movements, the more moderate advocates of international government appear to receive the strongest support from the American public. This is so much the case that *aspiration* for some form of effective international government—whether it take the form of the modification of the veto provisions of the United Nations charter or the formation of an Atlantic Federal Union—may be properly viewed as being a part of the present foreign policy consensus. Nevertheless, it is well to consider that the strength of these aspirations for international government has never been tested. Their genuineness may only be established when the economic and political sacrifices which would be imposed on Americans by participation in an international government would become unambiguously clear.

X. Consensus in a World of Crisis

THE "crisis of Western man" has become a common theme among learned men. Theologians decry the secularization of modern life, the decline of religious feeling, and the rise of materialism and "scientism." College presidents deplore the rise of vocationalism and the decay of humanist cultural ideals. Critics of the arts struggle against the domination of "mass" standards of taste and the crumbling of esthetic discrimination. Sociologists and social philosophers are troubled by the breakdown of older forms of community relations and the costs of urban industrial civilization in human isolation and insecurity. Business leaders and economists caution against the consequences of the decline of the risk-taking mentality and the emergence of security as a dominant social value. Psychiatrists and psycho-anthropologists comment on the competitiveness of modern life and the impairment of human relations which it entails. This is but a partial summary of the modern jeremiad.

One of the most interesting interpretations of the modern crisis of the spirit, an interpretation which brings into focus many of the problems with which we have thus far been concerned, is the "privatization" hypothesis of Ernst Kris and Nathan Leites. These writers propose that in the mass societies of the twentieth century, politics and public affairs have come to impinge ever more closely on the life of the common man. In a formal sense, the masses determine the basic political decisions which affect them, and they are encouraged by their leaders to believe that they actually exercise such power. But the complexity of modern economic and political decisions and the professionalization of the decision-making process has created the feeling that in actuality the masses can neither *"understand* nor *influence* the very events upon which their life and happiness is known to depend." [1] There has been, according to this view, an increasing sense of "incompetence" among the masses. Thus, in contrast to the era of political decentralization, when the average man is said to have had a sense of relatedness to, and understanding of, politics, contemporary Americans (and Western Europeans) have a sense of dependence upon, and distrust of, remote elites and decision-makers. This sense of powerlessness and suspicion is not discharged constructively in the form of "critical distrust" and critical evaluation of policy proposals and decisions. It cannot be expressed in constructive ways because the ordinary individual lacks the knowledge and analytical ability to evaluate policy in an age of complex interdependence. "He [the common man] therefore regressively turns to projective distrust: He fears, suspects and hates what he cannot understand and master." [2] He projects his own feelings of hostility and resentment, continually fed by his sense of powerlessness and of being a tool manipulated for purposes other than his own, on his leaders. In the mind of the common man the leadership groups become malevolent, cynical, self-seeking and corrupt. In conclusion, these writers suggest that if "the appropriate education on a vast enough scale and at a rapid enough rate is not provided for, the distrust and privatization of the masses may become a fertile soil for totalitarian management."

In the present state of knowledge it is impossible to accept or reject such a hypothesis. We have already seen that, particularly in relation to foreign policy, the feeling of powerlessness among Americans is widespread. But these feelings of powerlessness were most marked among the lower-income and lower-educational strata. They are less characteristic of the "attentive public" which feels itself capable of exercising in some measure the kind of "critical distrust" which represents a sound response to the modern political division of labor. Instead of withdrawing into private rancor and suspicion, the attentive public subjects policy to more- or less-informed criticism. Furthermore, with the broadening of educational opportunity and the general rise in the standard of living in the course of the past decades, it would seem that this attentive public has expanded.

It is indeed an arguable point as to whether Americans have been withdrawing from political involvement. In some areas we may perhaps speak of an increasing sense of political involvement and relatedness. Thus if we take the moral tone of American political life in the past half century, we find a genuine decline in the cruder forms of corruption and manipulation. The urban public of today is more effectively related to urban politics than was the case in the era of the "shame of the cities." But it is not related to politics in any direct sense of the term. It is related to politics through a *division of labor*. What broke the hold of the older and grosser forms of urban political corruption was the rise of effective civic elites capable of competing with the politicians, and the broadening of the attentive public through educational opportunity and rising standards of living.

There is a certain tendency to treat the nineteenth century in the United States as a utopian age of mass political involvement. Actually this was the era during which de Tocqueville called the United States "blessed" because it did not need a foreign policy. In his judgment, had the United States been involved in world politics, her survival would have been seriously threatened by the instability of the American democracy, its intense involvement in private affairs, and its proclivities for evangelistic interventions. The nineteenth century also was the era of the great waves of evangelism and complacency in urban politics. This was attributable to a kind of privatism which was perhaps stronger in the nineteenth century than it is today.

Actually political involvement in the United States in the era before the first world war tended to take the form either of evangelistic political religiosity or hard and narrow interest calculation. There was, as we have already seen, a certain cyclical fluctuation from the one mood to the other. What seems to be developing today is a disenchantment with all sweeping ideals and, in addition, a rejection of the older forms of narrow interest calculation. Thus in the first world war the United States joined the Allies in a mood of sweeping idealism. The disenchantment that followed in the next decade was in part a consequence of the collapse of these exorbitant hopes. In the second world war a more wary people rejected millennial aspirations. There was less willingness to accept general slogans and a greater resistance to propaganda. The mood responses of soldiers asked to fight,[3] and of civilians asked to sacrifice, were generally couched in simple terms of defense against aggression.

In this, as in other areas, there has undoubtedly been a decline in belief in general principles and ideals and a preference for interest calculation with the self as the starting point. But this tendency does not necessarily lead to political withdrawal and bitterness. It may lead into a broadening rationality in which the interdependence of individual and social action is recognized and in which there is a sober respect for the inevitability of division of labor in the making of complex policy decisions. Those writers who view the political apathy of the masses as a simple manifestation of social pathology have perhaps overlooked a number of essential aspects of the problem.

If we take any of the great problems of American foreign policy—such as the control of atomic energy, or the problem of Western European or Ear Eastern stability and security —we have to recognize that even the most highly trained specialists have to act in the dark and on the basis of anxious guess-work. There is indeed, as we have already stressed, a constructive sense of economy of effort in the reaction of the "common man" who refuses to involve himself and to accumulate knowledge about these problems. Would he be in any better position to evaluate policy if he were able to pass the information tests posed by the public opinion researchers? Suppose all adult Americans knew the name of their Secretary of State, could locate Iran on a blank map, could identify the raw materials from which fissionable materials are derived, and could list the permanent members of the Security Council in alphabetical order, could they then make a sound decision whether military aid under the North Atlantic Pact should be a billion dollars or a billion and a half? This approach to the problem of public information operates on a kind of "Quiz Kids" standard. Anyone who has gone through the experience of trying to analyze a policy is aware of the fact that in the first period of concentrated effort, increased knowledge results in increased confusion and indecision. Since the great mass of the public lacks the time, energy, and training necessary for more than the most superficial consideration of foreign policy problems, widespread mass ignorance and indifference are hardly to be viewed as simple pathologies.

Mass indifference toward problems of foreign policy is partly justified by the great proliferation of interest organizations in the past fifty years or so. The public is not only represented in the formal political sense by a variety of elected officials, but there are few groups of any size in the United States today which do not have their interest representation. *Mass inattention* to problems of public policy is accompanied by the *accentuation* of *elite attention*. The trade-union leader, the agricultural lobbyist or propagandist, the official of the Chamber of Commerce is "paid" to look out for the interests of the worker, farmer, or businessman. There is, undoubtedly, considerable distrust among the masses of their political and interest representation, a distrust which is largely sound and healthy. Pressure group leaders are agents, and there can be little question that they bear watching. Anyone who has had experience with agency relationships becomes aware of the constructive value of distrust and lack of confidence.

In the last half century the American population has developed a political structure adapted to an era of mass democracy and social interdependence. The implications of these developments have been accepted with great reluctance and in the form of an "under-the-counter" transaction. The myth of democratic spontaneity and mass control still holds sway "above the counter," only to trouble the literal minds of young people, and older people who have resisted the impact of experience.

These considerations are of significance for public information policy. Only recently an analysis of the results of a foreign information campaign in Cincinnati showed that even a heavy concentration of information through the mass media of communication had no perceptible effects.[4] According to the criteria used by the polling organization, approximately the same percentages of respondents were informed and ignorant after the campaign, as before.

What accounts for this mass immunity to information on foreign policy problems? The public information specialist who operates through the mass media reasons by analogy from the success of advertising. Advertisers get enormous results from radio, newspaper and periodical advertising, while information on the United Nations distributed through the same media appears to get no results at all. The point seems to be that the masses are already predisposed to want automobiles, refrigerators, and toothpaste, but they are not predisposed to want information about the United Nations or the control of atomic energy. Such information has no immediate utility or meaning.

What this and other studies suggest is that there is no mass market for detailed information on foreign affairs. The general public looks for *cues* for *mood responses* in public discussion of foreign policy. It does not listen to the content of discussion but to its tone. A presidential statement that a crisis exists will ordinarily be registered in the form of apprehension. A reassuring statement will be received with complacency reactions. In both cases the reaction has no depth and no structure.

But if there is no "quantity" market for information about foreign affairs, there is an important quality market. And it is through this quality market that an articulate and broad foreign policy consensus can be shaped and maintained. Through a disciplined democratic elite and a broad attentive public, foreign policy moods may be contained and gross fluctuations in attitude checked. No slick public relations campaign will "do the trick." The side-show barker who can appeal to well-established appetites will get the "cash," but little more than self-intoxication results from a grass roots campaign in Middletown, Ohio, "to relate Middletowners to the world in which we live." We are dealing with a complex political structure which has special points of access. If we shout at the wall, we can take a certain satisfaction in a ringing echo. But if we come up closer, we can find openings through which a quiet word might reach a listening ear.

An effective approach to public information on foreign policy questions will therefore be selective and qualitative. It will be directed toward enlarging the attentive public and training the elite cadres. This is not to suggest that the mass public is to be overlooked or neglected. A sound information program will confront the common man continually with opportunities to be informed and involved in foreign policy decisions. There should be a standing invitation for him to join the attentive public if and when he is ready to make the essential sacrifices of time and energy. The repetition of slogans and occasional promotional campaigns directed at the mass public through the mass media have the primary consequence of minimizing the complexities of the problem and encouraging self-deception.

The containment of mass moods and the broadening and qualitative improvement of the attentive public may be approximated through a bettering of elite selection and training. Our efforts ought to be directed toward the articulate points in the political structure. Both a democratic and effective foreign policy may be shaped and maintained as long as we have trained and disciplined elites competing for influence before an attentive public. These elites constitute an elaborate system of representation; they are (although in quite different ways and degrees) responsible to mass constituencies.

We have already referred to the shortcomings of the

various American elites—politicians, bureaucrats, pressure group leaders, journalists, social scientists, and the like. If we set as our standard of elite performance in foreign policy the objectives of democratic discipline, ideological consensus, and the development of a systematic and integrative mentality, we are led inevitably to the two primary training elites— the teachers and the clergy. These elites appear to fall short of fulfilling their tasks in a number of respects. Teachers and clergymen tend to be the bearers of moral and political idealism. They are susceptible to millennial hopes, and thereby lay the groundwork for cynical rejections and dis-illusionments among their charges. In this respect they con-tribute to American moral dualism; they are responsible in part for the persistence of instability in American opinion. They set up aspirations which cannot be fulfilled, and incul-cate principles of conduct which cannot be effective.

There is no short cut to the improvement of the educa-tional and religious elites. What might be proposed are such changes in the training of teachers and the clergy as will make it increasingly difficult for the practitioners of these professions to evade political reality. Few clergymen and teachers even in the purely formal sense study "politics." They are rarely called upon to confront the real problems of military and political security. An already strong penchant for escapism, which often lies at the basis of their choice of these professions, is encouraged by curricula badly adapted to the broad character-molding and ideal-setting function these elites are called on to perform.

It is the special task of the educational elites—and par-ticularly in higher education—to develop those analytical and integrative modes of thought so essential in policy-makers. The institutions of higher learning—and the social sciences in particular—have a potential function which cannot be sufficiently emphasized. The attentive public, as we have already seen, is largely a college-educated public, and the political, interest, and communications elites are also largely college trained. It is in the social sciences in the universities that a democratic ideological consensus can be fostered and a democratic elite discipline encouraged.

One of the factors responsible for the indiscipline of the democratic elites and for the persistence of ideological confusion, is the absence of a coherent theory of society and politics. The aim of such a theory would be to clarify the value premises and conflicts of the politically significant cultures and social groupings of our time. This is not to suggest that all conflicts will be resolved once the social sciences achieve a measure of theoretical clarity. What this would facilitate would be a type of discussion of public policy issues in which premises would be explicit and consequences of alternative policies comparatively clear. Developments in the social sciences in this direction would make it increasingly difficult for the policy and opinion elites to produce those magnificent inconsistencies, *non sequiturs*, and frequent elisions of logical analysis which confuse and obscure the public debate of important policy questions. A democratic discipline and a democratic consensus do not call for full and continuous agreement. What they require are a rational statement of the alternatives and a consensus as to the mode of selection among them. A homogeneous training in this kind of policy analysis might contribute to the development of a common language among the various elite sectors, a common method of problem-setting and problem-solving.

Among the interest elites perhaps the most important objective is to moderate the rigid assertion of narrow interest by the insight and analytical clarity of the specialist.

Sound interest representation is one of the most important methods of clarifying policy alternatives. The various interest positions can hardly be imagined in the detached study of the scholar, or adequately asserted by the politician who represents a heterogeneous constituency. The foreign policy orientations of interest groups would be greatly improved if these special points of view were screened through the minds of persons who have analytical familiarity with alternative foreign policies, persons who can set special interest advocacy in the context of social and political consequences. Efforts to foster such a development are hardly utopian, since the pressure groups themselves have begun to set the pattern of relying on specialists. It does not follow, of course, that the mere inclusion of such specialists will lead to a broader and more flexible conception of interest representation. Specialists, particularly where they have lost contact with their professions, often become mere interest advocates, using their skills to make more impressive cases for policies which have not been subjected to any analysis at all. Nevertheless, the presence of foreign policy specialists on the staffs of pressure groups cannot fail in the long run to make some improvement in the policy-making processes of these organizations. They introduce certain delays in action and complexities of insight and detail which act as barriers to the simple extension of group interest into the foreign policy arena. A sound information program on foreign policy will encourage this process of professionalization among the pressure group elites, will maintain continued contact with these specialists, and will endeavor to keep alive their professional standards.

This conception of professionalism—in the sense of the dignity of the calling—is the hallmark of a mature democratic elite. In a totalitarian society the elites acquire their dignity through the fulfillment of commands which in turn are derived from authoritative interpretations of the totalitarian mission. In this sense, they perform a duty which is specific and compulsory.

The democratic elites cannot appeal to this doctrine of authoritative mission and command. Though they are subject to the control of employers, the fluctuations of markets, and the choices of constituents, they have an area of discretion in defining their missions. There is room for conscience. From what sources do they derive their vocational criteria? The essence of the conception of professionalism—whether it be in politics, law, administration, journalism, scholarship, or the arts—is that the function of the particular calling sets certain standards of performance. Thus in journalism certain criteria flow from the task of providing information about significant events. Providing misinformation is a violation of the calling, just as a biased selection of information deviates from the standard of "getting out the news." It is not accidental that the controversies over the ethics of journalism turn on this question of whether the "news" has been fairly represented. Both the press and the critics of the press agree on the principle that the press has a *task*, and that this task involves giving a valid representation of significant events. The development of professionalism, as distinguished from the simple exercise of certain skills, involves this constant evaluation of performance according to the criteria set by the calling itself.

Thus we may say of the various foreign policy elites—in government, in the mass media, in academic life, and in the voluntary associations—that professionalism involves a constant search for the most adequate policy means to realize the values of their clienteles, whether they serve humanity,

238 THE AMERICAN PEOPLE AND FOREIGN POLICY

nations, social classes, religious movements, or age and sex groups.

If the intellectual and emotional energies of the elites are genuinely freed to pursue the implications of these value preferences, there comes a point where the values of humanity, nation, and class begin to converge, where common values begin to take their place beside the special ones. This is the "end of the rainbow" of the great rational consensual aspirations of Western man; it is to be sought in the modern era not by democratic spontaneity, but by democratic professionalism.

The dignity of the political calling rests on responsibility to the constituency, however this may be conceived, and to the values to which it aspires.[5] The dignity of the social-scientific calling rests on the clarification of value premises, the analysis of the adequacy of means, and the consequences of social action.[6] The dignity of the journalistic calling rests on the truthful representation of significant happenings. The dignity of the interest-group calling derives from the responsible representation of special interest in the context of political and social consequences. These elite values are more or less felt by those who perform these tasks. But the conditions affecting the exercise of these callings vary greatly in the degree of discretion left open to the individual practitioner. Perhaps the academic elites are least pressed with the urgency of routine and least restricted in the formulation of their goals. Those of us who would facilitate the development of this professionalism among the democratic elites will find that the starting point lies in the training of character and intellect. And a special responsibility attaches to those who have the task of interpreting man and his institutions to the new elite generations.

The argument so far advanced has had to do primarily

with the tactics of a public information program in the sphere of foreign affairs. It has suggested an approach through political structure rather than through mass campaigns, through qualitative changes at key points rather than through quantitative information. But what of the substantive problems of American opinion on foreign affairs?

Perhaps the gravest general problem confronting policy-makers is that of the instability of mass moods, the cyclical fluctuations which stand in the way of policy stability. Such stabilization may in part be achieved by the kind of elite discipline which has already been discussed. But there is evidence which suggests that the era of great fluctuations in American opinion may have passed, that some balance between the poles of American moods on foreign affairs may have been approximated. The comparative sobriety of American participation in World War II and the comparatively moderate decline in interest in foreign affairs in the postwar period substantiate such a hypothesis. Perhaps the contemporary American neither soars to such heights nor falls to such depths as has been the case in the past. The impact of historical experience has placed a ceiling on hopes and a floor on disappointment.

But even moderate fluctuations of moods may have serious consequences. While it is difficult to believe that the present readiness for foreign policy commitments will ever be supplanted by the kind of withdrawal which occurred after World War I, even a moderate return of complacency may seriously undermine the effectiveness of foreign policy. Such complacency affords opportunities to special interest elites to weaken the effect of foreign policy programs by the introduction of special exceptions and by penny-wise economies.

Thus the consequence of fluctuations in Soviet pressure may take the form of moderate American fluctuations in readiness to sacrifice. It is probably unrealistic to hope that such irrationalities in American foreign policy can be eliminated by any available means. On the other hand, there is a certain tendency to attribute to the Soviet elites a degree of policy discretion which their actual power situation is hardly likely to tolerate. To what extent and for what periods of time can the Soviet and Communist elites put on a conciliatory front without seriously weakening their own power position? American resolution cannot be greatly affected by mere verbal conciliation, and the Communists cannot accept a genuine stabilization without seriously weakening the dynamism and unity of their *movement.*

There are problems of American opinion which arise from the special attitudes and feelings of the various social groupings in the United States. The lower-income, unskilled labor, and the relatively uneducated groups present the most serious problems. These are the social groupings which seem to fit the "privatization" hypothesis of Kris and Leites. The evidence suggests that among the poor and ignorant of the cities and the countryside there are widespread feelings of powerlessness, of resentment, and bitterness, which produce a certain susceptibility to activist movements—whether they take the form of radical utopianism or reactionary nationalism. Democracy of participation and opportunity has never reached these elements in any adequate way. It is simple enough to say that we must reach these groups with propaganda and information, that we must lighten these dark areas of ignorance by short-run steps of one kind or another. All such direct approaches are bound to be of limited value at best. These groups lack both the motivation and the intellectual skills to make such information meaningful.

Only in the long-run and indirect ways can the lower-income groups be effectively related to American political life. This can be done through the spread of educational and social opportunity and the development of effective interest organization among them. The swift development of trade-union organization in the past fifteen years has produced elites and small attentive publics within certain sectors of this lower-income stratum. But there are still large groups which are inarticulate and unorganized—notably, the Negroes, the foreign born, and the rural poor. A sound democratic strategy would be directed at the creation of trained elites among these groups. But even these developments would represent a mere beginning. We should anticipate among these elites psychological phenomena quite comparable to the behavior of the new elites among the dependent peoples of the world. Only partly accepted in the established elite structure, they tend to be unstable, anxious, and insecure. They are, in the language of Kurt Lewin, "uncertain of their psychological ground." [7] Since these lower-income and lower-educational groups constitute so serious a problem, efforts at elite improvement and at establishing attentive strata should be concentrated in these areas. And yet, most of our efforts at present are directed toward the middle- and upper-class elements.

While it has been possible to identify an "attentive stratum" among the American public, relatively little is known about its dimensions and characteristics. We know that it is "informed" and that it possesses some of the details essential to the understanding of public policy; but the criteria employed are minimal and quantitative in character. We know that it is largely a college-educated stratum; but here again we have little information about its emotional and intellectual characteristics. The truth of the matter is that we know extremely little about the characteristics of the attentive public and the American elites save that they exist according to our criteria. An effective campaign directed toward stabilizing and articulating foreign policy moods requires thorough investigation and analysis before objectives and means can be established. The present analysis merely opens the problem for discussion.

The academic and religious elites have already been cited as the bearers of moral wishful thinking. The strata most susceptible to such thinking are the younger generations and women. Here again, quantitative campaigns through the mass media are of quite limited value. The approach has to be through the civic elites of the younger generations and the feminine organizational elites. Both of these groups are largely college products. If it were to become increasingly difficult for young people of either sex to complete their educations without confronting historical and political reality, the problem of youthful and feminine idealism might in part take care of itself.

The pessimism and bitterness among the older age groups is a problem of another order. It cannot be solved by intellectual training; it raises questions fundamental to American culture. American culture stresses instrumental knowledge, activism, accomplishment, success. The old in America, the potential bearers of mature wisdom, are pushed from the focus of attention as symbols of the meaninglessness of human effort and death. There is something deeply moving in the modern discovery of the neuroses of old age and in the utopian security movements of the older generations of the last twenty years. Such problems as these can only be resolved when the panic and urgency of American culture subside and honest relationships with tragedy and death are established.

Finally, we come to the shadow cast over human expectations through the discovery of the "unconventional" weapons of modern military technology. Since the beginning of the nineteenth century the physical security anxieties [8] of nations and peoples have risen, as their capacity for destruction has increased. By reason of geographic accident, Americans have been protected from the world struggle for power. They have tended to view the older peoples of the world as living in the fallen state of power politics. Americans now too have eaten of the forbidden fruit and have been driven from Eden. But they have registered the increased risks and costs of political life only in an oblique way. For reasons already discussed, they have repressed the personal meanings and implications of these developments.

The absence of overt concern should not conceal the fact that we are sitting on feelings of strong potential force which events may release with the most serious consequences. When the Soviet Union comes to the point of being able to reach the United States with modern weapons of destruction, the period of short-run American security will have run out. The psychological mechanisms which have produced a certain overt complacency in a world hardly suited to this mood will no longer control. Public opinion unprepared for the power game with such prohibitive stakes may either force premature decisions or delay timely ones.

There is, of course, a dilemma confronting efforts at preparing Americans for risks such as these. A premature mass campaign in the absence of an immediate threat might create "wolf, wolf" reactions, which would reduce the effectiveness of appeals at a later and more threatening time. At the same time, failure to prepare for these contingencies would leave us vulnerable to possible future panic.

Perhaps the wisest procedure at this stage of comparative American safety would be directed at the twofold aim of creating general public confidence that future contingencies are being planned for by the responsible agencies, and indoctrinating the elite groups in the military and civilian defense problems of the future. This is, perhaps, the only kind of psychological "fire drill" which is possible today. It might insure that possible future decisions will fall on a comparatively prepared public soil and that American policy will neither be forced nor restrained by the sudden welling of mass anxiety. A psychological policy for atomic war or threat of war cannot be effectively improvised. This is not at all to suggest that atomic war is inevitable. But anyone who would argue against such proposals for psychological preparation has the task of proving that there is no possibility whatever of atomic warfare.

There is a kind of hope which springs from the mastery of emotion and feeling, like that of the child who discovers that a frustration is bearable, or a terrifying risk within the scope of his competence. Such hope begins with the resistance of self-deception. It is as different from the willful selection of the favorable omen as it is from the protective selection of despair as a defense against disappointment. In this sense, the long road of foreign policy is not without hope. While it does not hold out the prospect of a joyous homecoming, a militant resistance to tyranny need not lead inevitably to disaster. History is full of examples of the crumbling of impressive façades.

It is human to aspire to a degree of security which is somehow commensurate to the risk. But if such security cannot be attained, we shall have to accept a lesser goal and live with our risks as best we can.

Notes

CHAPTER I

1. A term used in Thomas R. Adam, *Education for International Understanding*, Institute for Adult Education, New York, 1948.

CHAPTER III

1. Alexis de Tocqueville, *Democracy in America*, tr. by Phillips Bradley, Knopf, 1945, Vol. II, p. 136.

2. *Ibid.*, p. 141.

3. *Ibid.*, pp. 136-38.

4. *Ibid.*, pp. 134-35.

5. *Ibid.*, Vol. I, p. 235.

6. *Ibid.*, Vol. I, p. 234.

7. Francis J. Grund, *The Americans*, Marsh, Capen and Lyon, 1837, pp. 173-74. For similar views see Alexander Mackay, "Every American is an Apostle of The Democratic Creed" in *America in Perspective*, ed. by H. S. Commager, Random House, 1947, pp. 95 ff.

8. Grund, *op. cit.*, pp. 202-06.

9. Charles Dickens, *American Notes*, Dutton, 1934, pp. 242 ff.

10. Cited in Allan Nevins, *Americans Through British Eyes*, Oxford University Press, 1948, pp. 360 ff.

11. Richard Hofstadter, *Social Darwinism in American Thought 1860-1915*, University of Pennsylvania Press, 1945, Chapter II.

12. Nevins, *op. cit.*, p. 356.

13. James Bryce, *American Commonwealth*, Commonwealth Publishing Co., 1908, Vol. II, p. 307.

14. D. Riesman and N. Glazer, "Character Types and Political Apathy," *Research Project in Mass Communications*, Yale University, May 26, 1948.

15. Bryce, *op. cit.*, pp. 360-63.

16. *Ibid.*, p. 362.

17. *Ibid.*, p. 310.

18. M. Y. Ostrogorski, *Democracy and the Party System in the United States*, Macmillan, 1910, p. 399.

19. *Ibid.*, pp. 400-01.

20. *Ibid.*, pp. 409-10.

21. André Siegfried, *America Comes of Age*, Harcourt, Brace, 1927; D. W. Brogan, *Government of the People*, Harper, 1933; Brogan, *The American Problem*, London, 1944.

22. *Who Will be Master, Europe or America?*, Macaulay, 1927.

23. *Ibid.*, p. 189.

24. Cited in Allan Nevins, *op. cit.*, pp. 456 ff.

25. Harold Laski, *The American Democracy*, Viking Press, 1948, Chapters I and XIV. See also Ralph Barton Perry, *Characteristically American*, Knopf, 1949, Chapter I.

26. Commager, *op. cit.*, p. x ff.

27. Margaret Mead, *And Keep Your Powder Dry*, Morrow, 1943; Geoffrey Gorer, *The American People*, Norton, 1948; Clyde Kluckhohn and Florence R. Kluckhohn, "American Culture: Generalized Orientation and Class Patterns" in *Conflicts of Power in Modern Culture*, Seventh Symposium of Conference on Science, Philosophy and Religion, Harper, 1947, pp. 106-28; for a more general bibliography on psychocultural studies of national character see Nathan Leites, "Psycho-cultural Hypotheses About Political Acts," in *World Politics*, October, 1948, pp. 103 ff.

28. *The Neurotic Personality of Our Time*, Norton, 1937, pp. 281 ff.

29. *Ibid.*, p. 286.

30. *Escape from Freedom*, Farrar and Rinehart, 1941, pp. 270 ff.; *Man for Himself*, Rinehart and Co., 1947, pp. 67 ff. Fromm's concept of the "Marketing Orientation" is quite similar to Horney's concept of "competitiveness." Fromm similarly shows the connection between compulsive striving for external success and excessive demands for love and affection. See also the elaboration of the "marketing character" in David Riesman and Nathan Glazer's series of mimeographed memoranda on "Political Apathy and Character Structure" for the Committee on National Policy: *Research Project in Mass Communications*, Yale University, January 19, 1948, March 17, 1948, and May 26, 1948. Fromm's conception of the "marketing orientation" was partly anticipated in C. Wright Mills, "The Competitive Personality," *Partisan Review*, September-October, 1946, pp. 433 ff.

31. Gorer, *op. cit.*, p. 33.

32. *Ibid.*, p. 53.

33. *Ibid.*, p. 179.

34. C. and F. Kluckhohn, *loc. cit.* This paper also contains a running commentary by Martha Wolfenstein and Nathan Leites which elaborates some of the points made by the Kluckhohns, and suggests hypotheses as to child-rearing practices which might be associated with the various behavior tendencies described.

35. Clyde Kluckhohn, *Mirror for Man*, McGraw-Hill, 1949, pp. 241 ff.

36. For an excellent statement of the logical and methodological problems see Nathan Leites, *loc. cit.*, pp. 104 ff.

37. See the comment on this point by Wolfenstein and Leites in C. and F. Kluckhohn, *loc. cit.*, p. 109.

38. *Ibid.*, p. 111.

39. See among others Wallace Carroll's book on American propaganda policy during the war, *Persuade or Perish*, Houghton Mifflin, 1948. Apparently Roosevelt had in mind Grant's rather benevolent treatment of Lee at the time of the Southern surrender. But Roosevelt apparently never got around to explaining this to top advisers and administrators. Robert Sherwood in *Roosevelt and Hopkins* (Harper, 1948, pp. 696 ff.) makes the same point in detail.

40. Riesman and Glazer, *loc. cit.*, p. 9.

41. Lincoln Barnett, "God and the American People," *Ladies' Home Journal*, November, 1948, pp. 37 ff.

CHAPTER IV

1. Thomas A. Bailey, *The Man in the Street*, Macmillan, 1948, pp. 121 ff.

2. On the general question of the reliability of polling data see among others Hadley Cantril and Associates, *Gauging Public Opinion*, Princeton University Press, 1944, Parts One, Two, Three; Leonard Doob, *Public Opinion and Propaganda*, Holt, 1948, Chapters 6, 7, 8; Quinn McNemar, "Opinion-Attitude Methodology," *Psychological Bulletin*, July, 1946, pp. 562-69; Frederick Mosteller *et al.*, *The Pre-Election Polls of 1948*, Social Science Research Council, 1949.

3. National Opinion Research Center, *Cincinnati Looks at the United Nations*, 1948, pp. 5 ff.

4. Leonard S. Cottrell, Jr. and Sylvia Eberhart, *American Opinion on World Affairs in the Atomic Age*, Princeton University Press, 1948, pp. 95 ff.

5. National Opinion Research Center, *op. cit.*, pp. 12 ff.

6. "Dark Areas of Ignorance," *Public Opinion and Foreign Policy*, ed. by Lester Markel, Harper, 1949, p. 51. See also the studies of information on foreign affairs of the Survey Research Center, *Attitudes Toward United States-Russian Relations*, University of Michigan, December, 1948, pp. 62 ff.; *Public Attitudes Toward American Foreign Policy, Part I*, University of Michigan, May, 1947, pp. 34 ff.

7. National Opinion Research Center, *op. cit.*, pp. 6 ff.; Cottrell and Eberhart, *op. cit.*, pp. 94 ff.

8. Survey Research Center, *Attitudes Toward United States-Russian Relations*, p. 69.

9. See summaries and trend data on the decline of isolationism in Jerome S. Bruner, *Mandate from the People*, Duell, Sloan and Pearce, 1944, Chapter II; Hadley Cantril, "Opinion Trends in World War II," *Public Opinion Quarterly*, Spring, 1948, pp. 38 ff.; polls taken by the American Institute of Public Opinion in the period January, 1942, through August, 1947, when the question, "Which of these two things do you think the U.S. should try to do when the war is over—stay out of world affairs or take an active part in world affairs?" elicited support for active participation which at no time fell below 60 per cent.

10. Bruner, *op. cit.*, pp. 41 ff.; National Opinion Research Center, *op. cit.*, pp. 8 ff.

CHAPTER V

1. National Opinion Research Center (hereafter abbreviated NORC), poll sent out June 18, 1943.

2. American Institute of Public Opinion (hereafter abbreviated AIPO), poll sent out February 20, 1945.

3. NORC, poll sent out July, 1945.

4. AIPO, release date, July 30, 1948.

5. See Survey Research Center (hereafter abbreviated SRC), *Attitudes Toward United States-Russian Relations*, University of Michigan, December, 1948, pp. 35 ff.

6. 34.2 per cent believed Russia to be the worst influence as compared to 55.3 per cent who believed Germany to be the worst. *Fortune* poll, release date, March, 1940.

7. Bruner, *op. cit.*, chart facing p. 109.

8. NORC, poll sent out January 5, 1942.

9. *Fortune* poll, release date, January, 1945.

10. NORC, poll sent out January, 1945.

11. *Fortune* poll, release date, September, 1945.

12. AIPO, poll sent out March, 1945.

13. *Fortune* poll, release dates, September, 1945; July, 1946; October, 1947.

14. SRC, *Attitudes Toward United States-Russian Relations*, pp. 34 ff.

15. See the series of polls of the National Opinion Research Center sent out December, 1944, and January, February, April, and May of 1945.

16. February and September. These observations are based on thirty-two surveys conducted by the National Opinion Research Center, the American Institute of Public Opinion, and the Office of Public Opinion Research of Princeton University. The results for the period 1942-44 are reported in a trend chart in Bruner, *op. cit.*, facing page 111.

17. AIPO, release date, May 3, 1948.

18. Release date, June, 1948.

19. NORC, surveys sent out August, 1942; November, 1942; February, 1943; June, 1943; November, 1943; September, 1944; November, 1944; December, 1944; and March, 1945.

20. NORC.

21. Roper poll, New York *Herald Tribune*, May 3, 1945.

22. NORC, *The Public Looks at World Organization*, University of Denver, 1944, p. 16.

23. Surveys sent out March 13, 1946, July 24, 1946, and March 3, 1948.

24. AIPO, surveys sent out August, 1947; February, 1948.

25. Results of the survey, conducted in the early spring of 1948, are published by *Time* in a report *Where Stands Freedom?*, April, 1948.

26. This figure is based on a series of sixteen American Institute of Public Opinion polls made within the period December, 1942, to April, 1948.

27. AIPO, survey sent out February 4, 1948.

28. AIPO, release dates, February 25, 1949; March 28, 1949; May 18, 1949; July 8, 1949.

29. See AIPO release of February 25, 1949.

30. AIPO, release dates, May 27, 1949, and July 10, 1949.

31. See Cottrell and Eberhart, *op. cit.*, p. 14.

32. Cornell University, *Public Reaction to the Atomic Bomb and World Affairs*, April, 1947, pp. 99 ff.

33. Cottrell and Eberhart, *op. cit.*, Appendix B.

34. NORC, surveys sent out in February and October, 1947; 51 per cent in favor in February, and 55 per cent in October.

35. AIPO, surveys sent out May 27, 1948.

36. Thirty-nine per cent in February, 1947, and 40 per cent in October, 1947.

37. NORC, survey sent out October, 1947.

38. NORC, survey sent out October, 1947.

39. NORC, survey sent out September, 1945.

40. Release date, December, 1945.

41. NORC, survey sent out March, 1946.

42. AIPO, release date, August 8, 1949.

CHAPTER VI

1. See, for example, M. Brewster Smith, "The Personal Setting of Public Opinions," *Public Opinion Quarterly*, Winter, 1947-48, pp. 507 ff.; Donald W. MacKinnon, "The Use of Clinical Method in Social Psychology," *The Journal of Social Issues*, November, 1946, pp. 47 ff.

2. Arthur Kornhauser, "Experience with a Poll of Experts," *Public Opinion Quarterly*, Fall, 1948, pp. 399 ff.; F. Stuart Chapin, "Mass Versus Leadership; Opinion on Wartime Rationing," *Public Opinion*

Quarterly, Winter, 1947-48, pp. 581 ff. Some of these theoretical problems are raised in Avery Leiserson, "Opinion Research and the Political Process," *Public Opinion Quarterly,* Spring, 1949, pp. 39 ff.; Benjamin H. Williams, "Public Opinion in a World of Power Politics," *Public Opinion Quarterly,* Fall, 1947, pp. 360 ff.; Lindsay Rogers, *The Pollsters,* Knopf, 1949, pp. 18 ff.; David B. Truman, "Political Behavior and Voting," in Frederick Mosteller *et al., op. cit.,* pp. 225-50.

3. NORC, *UNESCO And Public Opinion Today,* University of Chicago, 1947, p. 39.

4. *Ibid.,* p. 42.

5. *Fortune,* September, 1948.

6. SRC, *Attitudes Toward United States-Russian Relations,* University of Michigan, December, 1948, p. 71.

7. NORC, *The Public Looks at Trade and Tariff Problems,* University of Chicago, p. 28.

8. SRC, *Public Attitudes Toward American Foreign Policy,* University of Michigan, May, 1947, Part II, p. 82.

9. SRC, *Public Attitudes Toward Russia and United States-Russian Relations,* University of Michigan, March, 1947, Part I, Table 22.

10. SRC, *Attitudes Toward United States-Russian Relations,* October, 1948, p. 83.

11. NORC, *Can The U.N.O. Prevent Wars?,* University of Denver, 1946, p. 10.

12. SRC, *Public Reaction to the Atomic Bomb and World Affairs,* University of Michigan, February, 1947, Table I-34.

13. SRC, *Public Attitudes Toward Russia and United States-Russian Relations,* University of Michigan, Part I, Table 7.

14. Geoffrey Gorer, *op. cit.,* pp. 50 ff.

15. Richard Centers, *The Psychology of Social Classes,* Princeton University Press, 1949.

16. In addition to the figures reported in Table I which are based on Gallup, NORC, and *Fortune* findings, see the various SRC reports cited above.

17. See Martin Kriesberg, "Dark Areas of Ignorance," in *Public Opinion and Foreign Policy,* ed. by Lester Markel, Harper, 1949.

18. NORC, *UNESCO and Public Opinion Today,* University of Chicago, p. 43.

19. SRC, *Public Reaction to the Atomic Bomb and World Affairs,* University of Michigan, Table I-34.

20. *Ibid.,* Table I-46.

21. NORC, *UNESCO and Public Opinion Today,* University of Chicago, p. 71.

22. SRC, *Public Reaction to the Atomic Bomb and World Affairs,* University of Michigan, Table I-34.

23. *Ibid.*, Table I-46.

24. NORC, *UNESCO and Public Opinion Today*, University of Chicago, p. 43.

25. Karl Mannheim, *Man and Society in an Age of Reconstruction*, Harcourt, Brace, 1940, pp. 58 ff.

26. The presence of this feeling of powerlessness among the lower-income groups is brought out again and again in the excellent series of reports on public attitudes toward foreign affairs issued by the SRC, University of Michigan. See particularly *Public Attitudes Toward Russia and United States-Russian Relations*, Part I, Appendix.

27. NORC, *The Public Looks at Trade and Tariff Problems*, University of Chicago, p. 19.

28. *Ibid.*, p. 28.

29. For evidence of this reluctance to express an opinion see particularly the following polls: SRC, *Public Attitudes Toward Russia and United States-Russian Relations*, Part I, Tables 5 and 16; SRC, *Public Attitudes Toward American Foreign Policy*, Part II, Table 35; NORC, *UNESCO and Public Opinion Today*, p. 43.

30. SRC, *Public Attitudes Toward Russia and United States-Russian Relations*, Part I, Appendix A, Table 14.

CHAPTER VII

1. Pareto's theory of the elite is fully treated in the introduction to his *Les Systemes Socialistes*, Paris, 1902, pp. 1-73.

2. *Ibid.*, p. 2.

3. Harold D. Lasswell, *Power and Personality*, Norton, 1948, pp. 108 ff.

4. See Thomas A. Bailey, *The Man in the Street*, Macmillan, 1948, Chapter I; Lester Markel, ed., *Public Opinion and Foreign Policy*, Harper, 1949, particularly Chapters I, II, XI; Bertrand Russell, M. Q. Sibley, Nathaniel Peffer, Max Kempelman, and C. Hartley Grattan, "Can Foreign Policy Be Democratic?", *American Perspective*, September, 1948, pp. 147-81.

5. See Paul F. Lazarsfeld, Bernard Berelson, and Hazel Gaudet, *The People's Choice*, Columbia University Press, 1948; Edward A. Shils and Morris Janowitz, "Cohesion and Disintegration in the Wehrmacht," *Public Opinion Quarterly*, Summer, 1948, pp. 280 ff.

6. For a similar view in relation to our China policy see Nathan Leites and David Nelson Rowe, "Choice in China," *World Politics*, April, 1949, p. 307.

7. *The Politics of Democracy*, Norton, 1940, pp. 134 ff.

8. See George F. Kennan's excellent analysis of the demands of the foreign service on character and intellect, "The Needs of the Foreign

Service," in *The Public Service and University Education*, ed. by Joseph E. McLean, Princeton University Press, 1949, pp. 97 ff.

9. See for example, Alfred S. Cleveland, "N.A.M. Spokesman for Industry," *Harvard Business Review*, May, 1948; Eli Ginzberg, *The Labor Leader*, Macmillan, 1948, p. 54.

10. The Commission on Freedom of the Press, *A Free and Responsible Press*, University of Chicago Press, 1947, p. 55.

11. Llewellyn White, *The American Radio*, University of Chicago Press, 1947, p. 213.

12. Ruth A. Inglis, *Freedom of the Movies*, University of Chicago Press, 1947, pp. 8 ff. For a comparative analysis of American and German movie plots see Donald V. McGranahan and Ivor Wayne, "German and American Traits Reflected in Popular Drama," *Human Relations*, July, 1948, particularly pp. 437 ff.

13. On this general problem see Harold D. Lasswell, *Power and Personality*, Norton, 1948, Chapter VI.

14. For a more comprehensive discussion of these criteria see Frederick S. Dunn, "The Scope of International Relations," *World Politics*, Vol. I, No. 1, pp. 142 ff., and "Education and Foreign Affairs," in *The Public Service and University Education*, ed. by Joseph E. McLean, Princeton University Press, 1949.

15. The generalizations which follow are based on an analysis of the leading articles dealing with foreign affairs appearing in four general political science journals—*Political Science Quarterly*, *The Journal of Politics*, *The American Political Science Review*, and *The Review of Politics*—for the period 1946-48 and the first quarter of 1949. Had such specialized international relations journals as the *Journal of International Law* and *International Organization* been included, the findings would have been even less satisfactory from the point of view of our criteria.

CHAPTER VIII

1. Max Weber, *The Theory of Social and Economic Organization*, tr. by A. M. Henderson and Talcott Parsons, Oxford University Press, 1947, pp. 115 ff.

2. Congress of Industrial Organizations, *Daily Proceedings of the Ninth Constitutional Convention*, October 15, 1947, pp. 39 ff., pp. 59 ff.

3. See statement of James B. Carey, *North Atlantic Treaty: Hearings before the Committee on Foreign Relations, U.S. Senate*, 81st Congress, 1st Session, pp. 413-15.

4. Congress of Industrial Organizations, *1948 Proceedings*, pp. 228 ff.

5. *Ibid.*

6. American Federation of Labor, *Report of the Proceedings of the Sixty-Sixth Convention*, pp. 176 ff.

7. *Ibid.*, pp. 482-83, p. 486.

8. *Ibid.*, pp. 450-51.

9. *Reciprocal Trade Agreements Program: Hearings before the Ways and Means Committee, House of Representatives,* 80th Congress, 1st Session, p. 1835; in contrast see the testimony of James B. Carey of the CIO on pp. 2375 ff.

10. *Ibid.*, p. 2387.

11. United States Chamber of Commerce, *Foreign Commerce Policies of the Chamber of Commerce of the United States,* 1946, p. 22.

12. Chamber of Commerce of the United States, *Aid to Europe,* November 21, 1947, p. 7.

13. *Ibid.*, p. 8. For a later Chamber of Commerce position on ERP see *Business Action,* "Report of the 36th Annual Meeting of the Chamber of Commerce of the U.S.," May 7, 1948, pp. 19 ff.

14. See statement of John Ben Shepperd, *European Recovery Program: Hearings before the Committee on Foreign Relations, U.S. Senate,* 80th Congress, 2nd Session, p. 1028.

15. See statement of Robert J. Bishop for the U.S. Junior Chamber of Commerce, *The Structure of the United Nations and the Relations of the United States to the United Nations: Hearings before the Committee on Foreign Affairs, House of Representatives,* 80th Congress, 2nd Session, pp. 420-24.

16. Research Committee of the Committee for Economic Development, *International Trade, Foreign Investment, and Domestic Employment,* June, 1945, p. 13.

17. Statement of Ralph E. Flanders, *Reciprocal Trade Agreements Program: Hearings before the Ways and Means Committee, House of Representatives,* 80th Congress, 1st Session, p. 2398.

18. Research and Policy Committee of the Committee for Economic Development, *An American Program of European Economic Cooperation,* February, 1948, pp. 12 ff.

19. See Alfred S. Cleveland, "N.A.M. Spokesman for Industry," *Harvard Business Review,* May, 1948.

20. Testimony of Francis L. Hopkinson on behalf of NAM, *Reciprocal Trade Agreements Program: Hearings before the Ways and Means Committee, House of Representatives,* 80th Congress, 1st Session, p. 2597.

21. This position was stated in the NAM testimony during House-Senate Hearings on the ECA, and repeated in the most recent policy statements of the NAM. See National Association of Manufacturers, *Industry Believes: Association Policies Adopted by the Board and Resolutions Passed at the Annual Congress of American Industry,* February, 1949, p. 36.

22. American Farm Bureau Federation, *Resolutions Adopted at the 30th Annual Convention,* December 16, 1948, p. 5.

23. National Grange, *A Résumé of Agricultural Policy, 82nd Ses-*

sion, November, 1948, p. 16; testimony of J. T. Sanders, *Universal Military Training: Hearings before the Committee on Armed Services, U.S. Senate*, 80th Congress, 2nd Session, pp. 151-60.

24. National Grange, *A Résumé of Agricultural Policy, 82nd Session*, p. 17.

25. National Grange, *Statement of Albert S. Goss, Master of the National Grange before the Resolutions Committee of the Republican National Convention*, June 17, 1948.

26. Testimony of J. T. Sanders, *European Recovery Program: Hearings before the Committee on Foreign Relations, U.S. Senate*, 80th Congress, 2nd Session, pp. 1119-28.

27. The Farmers Union is treated in detail in the following chapter.

28. The American Legion, *Digest of Minutes of the National Executive Committee*, May, 1948, p. 80.

29. Veterans of Foreign Wars, *Press Release*, November 17, 1947.

30. *Ibid.*, December 20, 1947.

31. AMVETS, *Minutes of the National Executive Committee Meeting*, April 3-4, 1948; AMVETS, *Digest of 1948 AMVET Objectives* (mimeo.).

32. *The AVC Bulletin: AVC Platform Supplement*, August, 1947, p. 4.

33. AVC Resolutions, adopted February 28, 1948 (mimeo.).

34. *Ibid.*, Appendix D.

35. Testimony of Gilbert A. Harrison, *North Atlantic Treaty: Hearings before the Committee on Foreign Relations, U.S. Senate*, 81st Congress, 2nd Session, pp. 917-25.

36. AVC Resolutions, *op. cit.*, Appendix B.

37. Lucille Cardin Crain and Anne Burrows Hamilton, "Packaged Thinking for Women," *American Affairs*, October, 1948 (supplement).

38. General Federation of Women's Clubs, *Resolutions Adopted in Convention, Portland, Oregon*, May 24-29, 1948.

39. See statement of Mrs. Frederic Beggs, *North Atlantic Treaty: Hearings before the Committee on Foreign Relations, U.S. Senate*, 81st Congress, 1st Session, pp. 597-607.

40. See statement of Miss Anna Lord Strauss, *Assistance to Greece and Turkey: Hearings before the Committee on Foreign Affairs, House of Representatives*, 80th Congress, 1st Session, pp. 273-276.

41. Statement of Mrs. Kathryn H. Stone, *North Atlantic Treaty: Hearings before the Committee on Foreign Relations, U.S. Senate*, 81st Congress, 1st Session, p. 594.

42. National Federation of Business and Professional Women's Clubs, *Legislative Platform, 1948-49;* see also statement of Olive H. Huston, *Universal Military Training: Hearings before the Committee on Armed Services, U.S. Senate*, 80th Congress, 2nd Session, p. 511.

43. See statement of Professor Mildred Northrop, *Reciprocal Trade*

*Agreements Program: Hearings before the Ways and Means Committee,
House of Representatives,* 80th Congress, 1st Session, pp. 432 ff.

44. *Resolutions Adopted by the Women's Action Committee for Lasting Peace,* April 7-9, 1948, p. 1; see also Women's Action Committee
for Lasting Peace, *Proposed International Plank to be Submitted to the
Political Conventions in 1948* (mimeo.).

45. *North Atlantic Treaty: Hearings before the Committee on Foreign Relations, U.S. Senate,* 81st Congress, 1st Session, p. 624.

46. New York *Times,* May 1, 1948.

47. See statement of Walter W. Van Kirk, *Universal Military Training: Hearings before the Committee on Armed Services, U.S. Senate,*
80th Congress, 2nd Session, pp. 511-15.

48. Federal Council of Churches of Christ in America, *Minutes of the
Executive Committee,* March 25, 1947, p. 6.

49. Federal Council of Churches of Christ in America, *Actions by the
Federal Council in Support of the Reciprocal Trade Agreements Program,* May 14, 1948 (mimeo.).

50. Dr. Helen C. Potter, *The Marshall Plan,* C.A.I.P. Pamphlet No.
40, Washington, D. C., 1948, p. 47.

51. Sister Thomasine, O.P., *The International Trade Organization,*
C.A.I.P. Pamphlet No. 42, Washington, D. C., 1948.

52. Letter from the Catholic Association for International Peace,
*North Atlantic Treaty: Hearings before the Committee on Foreign Rela-
tions, U.S. Senate,* 81st Congress, 1st Session, p. 1193.

53. These data are adapted from material on file at The Common
Council for American Unity, 1947. See also Yaroslav J. Chyz and Reed
Lewis, "Agencies Organized by Nationality Groups in the United States,"
Annals of the American Academy of Political and Social Science, March,
1949.

54. Thomas A. Bailey, *The Man in the Street,* Macmillan, 1948, pp.
20 ff.

55. *European Recovery Program: Hearings before the Committee on
Foreign Relations, U.S. Senate,* 80th Congress, 2nd Session, p. 1250.

56. See New York *Times,* December 27, 1948.

57. See American Zionist Emergency Council, press release, June 18,
1948.

58. See, for example, the *Council News* and a series of pamphlets issued on the Palestine question; for a statement of Council policies see
The American Council for Judaism: Its Principles and Program,
adopted at Fourth Annual Conference, February 19, 1948.

59. New York *Times,* October 21, 1948.

60. Louis Bean, *How to Predict Elections,* Knopf, 1948, pp. 96 ff.

61. New York *Times,* April 12, 1948; *Resolution Presented to the*

Resolutions Committee of the Republican National Convention, June 18, 1948.

62. Common Council for American Unity, cited above.

63. Survey Research Center, *Public Attitudes Toward American Foreign Policy,* May, 1947, p. 16.

64. Florence B. Widutis, "The Impact of Citizen Organizations in Public Opinion and Public Policy," *International Journal of Opinion and Attitude Research,* December, 1947, pp. 63 ff.

65. Some two-thirds of the respondents in a recent Gallup poll approved the North Atlantic Treaty. See AIPO, release date, July 8, 1949.

66. Survey Research Center, *American Attitudes Toward Aid to Europe,* January, 1948, pp. 7 ff.

CHAPTER IX

1. *North Atlantic Treaty: Hearings before the Committee on Foreign Relations, U.S. Senate,* 81st Congress, 1st Session, p. 473.

2. *Congressional Record,* 80th Congress, 2nd Session, Vol. 94, Part 2, p. 2393.

3. Survey Research Center, *Attitudes Toward United States-Russian Relations,* December, 1948, pp. 32-34.

4. *Ibid.,* p. 26.

5. *Ibid.,* p. 27.

6. *European Recovery Program: Hearings before the Committee on Foreign Relations, U.S. Senate,* 80th Congress, 2nd Session, pp. 890 ff.

7. Walter Linn, *Dangers to Our American Way of Life,* National Economic Council, March, 1947.

8. Statement of Merwin K. Hart, *Universal Military Training: Hearings before the Committee on Armed Services, U.S. Senate,* 80th Congress, 2nd Session, p. 1092.

9. Speech of Merwin K. Hart over the ABC Network, February 23, 1948.

10. National Economic Council, *Economic Council Letter,* No. 167, May 15, 1947.

11. Statement of Dr. H. M. Griffith, *North Atlantic Treaty: Hearings before the Committee on Foreign Relations, U.S. Senate,* 81st Congress, 1st Session, pp. 851 ff.

12. *European Recovery Program: Hearings before the Committee on Foreign Relations, U.S. Senate,* 80th Congress, 2nd Session, p. 1276.

13. American Coalition, *Resolutions Adopted at its Annual Convention in Washington, D. C.,* January 27, 1949.

14. John B. Trevor, *The Foreign Alliance,* American Coalition, Washington, D. C., May, 1949, p. 14.

15. American Institute of Public Opinion, release date, November 28, 1948.

16. American Institute of Public Opinion, release dates, February 25, 1949; March 28, 1949; May 11, 1949; May 16, 1949; May 18, 1949; July 8, 1949.

17. American Institute of Public Opinion, release date, May 11, 1949.

18. Survey Research Center, *Attitudes Toward United States-Russian Relations*, December, 1948, pp. 5 ff., and *American Attitudes Toward Aid to Europe*, January, 1948, p. 1.

19. For a brief treatment of the theological bases of the different varieties of religious pacifism, see The Pacifist Research Bureau, "Conscientious Objectors in World War II," *Quarterly Research Survey*, January, 1949, pp. 2-3.

20. Milton Mayer, "They Witness Against Thee," *Fellowship*, July, 1949, p. 13.

21. Report released by the Friends Service Committee, New York *Times*, July 18, 1949.

22. Friends Committee on National Legislation, *Memorandum of Interest to Religious Groups*, March 23, 1949.

23. Statement of A. Stauffer Curry, *North Atlantic Treaty: Hearings before the Committee on Foreign Relations, U.S. Senate*, 81st Congress, 1st Session, pp. 836 ff.

24. An exception is Peacemakers, a small organization of some five hundred members. Fifty of its members of draft age are in prison for refusal to register for the draft.

25. Statement of Dr. Phillips Elliott, *North Atlantic Treaty: Hearings before the Committee on Foreign Relations, U.S. Senate*, 81st Congress, 2nd Session, pp. 756-57.

26. Post War World Council, *News Bulletin*, January, 1948, p. 6. See also Norman Thomas' restatement of this position in New York *Times*, July 27, 1949.

27. Socialist Party Platform for 1948.

28. National Farmers Union supplement, *Program of the National Farmers Union Adopted by the National Convention*, March, 1948; see also statement of Russell Smith, *Reciprocal Trade Agreements Program: Hearings before the Ways and Means Committee, House of Representatives, 80th Congress, 1st Session.*

29. Statement of Russell Smith, *Assistance to Greece and Turkey: Hearings before the Committee on Foreign Affairs, House of Representatives*, 80th Congress, 1st Session, p. 312.

30. There are, in addition, pacifists who are isolationist in principle. The National Council for Prevention of War is the best example of this point of view.

31. For the general views of the Hutchins group, see their periodical *Common Cause: A Journal of One World.*

32. New York *Times*, March 21, 1948.

33. *Ibid.*

34. *Ibid.*, January 27, 1949.

35. See editorial in *Common Cause*, "Big Two Meeting and the Atlantic Pact," April, 1949, pp. 321 ff.

36. Cord Meyer, Jr., "The Search for Security," address at a luncheon forum sponsored by the United World Federalists and The Federation of American Scientists, Washington, D. C., April 19, 1947.

37. W. T. Holliday (Vice President of United World Federalists), "Our Final Choice," *Reader's Digest*, January, 1948.

38. Statement of Cass Canfield (Chairman of the Executive Committee, United World Federalists), *North Atlantic Treaty: Hearings before the Committee on Foreign Relations, U.S. Senate*, 81st Congress, 1st Session, pp. 841-42.

39. See statement of Ely Culbertson, *Structure of the United Nations and the Relations of the United States to the United Nations: Hearings before the Committee on Foreign Affairs, House of Representatives*, 80th Congress, 2nd Session, pp. 482 ff.

40. Statement of Clarence Streit to The Resolutions Committee of The Republican National Convention, June 18, 1948.

41. See speech of Senator Estes Kefauver, *Congressional Record*, 81st Congress, 1st Session, Vol. 95, pp. 9388 ff.; see also statement of Owen J. Roberts, *North Atlantic Treaty: Hearings before the Committee on Foreign Relations, U. S. Senate*, 81st Congress, 1st Session, p. 535, also statement of Robert P. Patterson, p. 612.

42. AIPO, surveys sent out July 24, 1946; August 14, 1946; August 1, 1947.

CHAPTER X

1. E. Kris and N. Leites, "Trends in Twentieth Century Propaganda," in *Psychoanalysis and the Social Sciences*, 1947, pp. 393 ff.

2. *Ibid.*, p. 402.

3. Samuel A. Stouffer *et al.*, *The American Soldier: Adjustment During Army Life*, Princeton University Press, 1949, Vol. I, pp. 431 ff.

4. NORC, *Cincinnati Looks at the United Nations*, Report 37; *Cincinnati Looks Again*, Report 37A.

5. H. H. Gerth and C. Wright Mills, *From Max Weber: Essays in Sociology*, Oxford University Press, 1946, pp. 77 ff.

6. *Ibid.*, pp. 129 ff.

7. Kurt Lewin, *Resolving Social Conflicts*, Harper, 1948, pp. 145 ff.

8. John Herz, "Idealist Internationalism and the Security Dilemma," in forthcoming issue of *World Politics*.

Index

A

Academic elites. *See* Elites
Adam, Thomas R., 245 *n.*
Aggression, attitude toward in America, 44. *See also* Communist
Agricultural organizations, 150, 168-71
Air force, American, 16, 104, 172
Albania, 72
Allies: World War I, 66, 229; World War II, 131
American Coalition of Patriotic Societies. *See* Patriotic
American Council of Christian Churches. *See* Christian
American Council for Judaism. *See* Judaism
American Farm Bureau Federation. *See* Farm
American Federation of Labor, 160, 252 *n.*
American Institute of Public Opinion. *See* Public
American Labor Party. *See* Labor
American Legion, 171, 254 *n.*
American Political Science Review, 252 *n.*
American-Soviet Friendship, National Council of, 196
American Veterans Committee. *See* Veterans
American Wage Earners Protective Conference. *See* Wage
American Zionist Emergency Council. *See* Zionist

AMVETS, 171-72, 254 *n.*
Ancient Order of Hibernians, 185
Anthropologists, 40
Anti-intellectualism, American, 46, 56
Apathy, 53; factors affecting, 8. *See also* Lower-income groups
Appeasement, 195-200, 224
Arab states, 188
Army, 104
Arnold, Matthew, 34
Arrogance, American, 64
Artists, 64
Arts and Sciences, National Council of, 196
Assembly, United Nations. *See* United Nations
Atlantic Union Committee for a Federal Convention, 222-23
Atomic attack, American defense against, 108; preventive, 115
Atomic bomb, 77, 81, 107, 133, 218
Atomic energy, 81, 222, 230; control of, 172; international control of, 111
Atomic war, 15, 244
Atomic weapons, 15, 16, 106-15; Russian, 109
Atomization, American, 48
Attentive public, 139, 151, 228, 233
Attitude surveys, 116
Attitudes: American, 8; toward Russia, 92-99
Authoritarianism, 20, 26
Authority in America, 51-53

B

Backus, Mrs. Dana C., 178
Bailey, Thomas A., 247 *n.*, 251 *n.*, 255 *n.*
Balance of power, 11, 14
Barkley, Alben, 200-202
Barnett, Lincoln, 247 *n.*
Bean, Louis, 187, 255 *n.*
Beggs, Mrs. Frederic, 254 *n.*
Benelux agreements, 212
Berelson, Bernard, 251 *n.*
Berlin: blockade, 78, 105, 120, 160; crisis, 18, 92
"Big Three," 96
Bishop, Robert J., 253 *n.*
Bohemia, 72
Brethren Service Commission, 212
Brogan, Dennis W., 38, 246 *n.*
Bruner, Jerome S., 248 *n.*
Bryce, James, 35, 38, 245 *n.*
Bureaucrats, 234
Business and Professional Women's Clubs, National Federation of, 175, 177, 254 *n.*
Business: cycle, 65, 68; organizations, 150, 163-68
Byrnes, James, 77, 149

C

Canada, 182
Canfield, Cass, 258 *n.*
Cantril, Hadley, 247 *n.*
Capitalism, 159; free-enterprise, 26
Carey, James B., 252 *n.*
Carroll, Wallace, 247 *n.*
Catholic Association for International Peace, 179, 181, 255 *n.*
Catholic Church, 179, 181, 208
Catholic Welfare Conference, National, 181
Centers, Richard, 122, 250 *n.*

Chamber of Commerce, United States, 163-164, 177, 253 *n.*
Chamber of Commerce, United States Junior, 165
Chapin, F. Stuart, 249 *n.*
Charter, United Nations. *See* United Nations
China, 115, 150, 173; Communism in, 85, 105
Christian Association, Young Women's, 177
Christian Churches, American Council of, 180
Christian pacifism. *See* Pacifism
Christianity, 34, 45, 52
Church of the Brethren, 212
Churches of Christ in America, Federal Council of, 179, 255 *n.*
Chyz, Yaroslav J., 255 *n.*
Cincinnati, public opinion study in. *See* Public opinion
Citizen's Committee for United Nations Reform. *See* United Nations
Clayton, Will, 223
Clergy, 100, 234
Cleveland, Alfred S., 252 *n.*, 253 *n.*
Cold War, 22, 67, 78
Colonial Lords of the Manor, Order of, 205
Columnists, 151
Cominform, 77
Commager, Henry Steele, 39, 245 *n.*
Committee for Economic Development. *See* Economic
Common Council for American Unity, 255 *n.*, 256 *n.*
Communication, 141. *See also* Elites
Communism, 13, 18, 93, 170, 193, 203, 211, 216; Leninist-Stalinist, 147